Anti-Asian Violence
in No

Critical Perspectives on Asian Pacific Americans Series

Books in the series will educate and inform readers in the academy, in Asian American communities, and the general public regarding Asian Pacific American experiences. They examine key social, economic, psychological, cultural, and political issues. Theoretically innovative, engaging, comparative, and multidisciplinary, these books reflect the contemporary issues that are of critical importance to understanding and empowering Asian Pacific Americans.

Series Titles Include

Diana Ting Liu Wu, *Asian Pacific Americans in the Workplace* (1997)

Juanita Tamayo Lott, *Asian Americans: From Racial Category to Multiple Identities* (1997)

Jun Xing, *Asian America through the Lens: History, Representations, and Identity* (1998)

Pyong Gap Min and Rose Kim, editors, *Struggle for Ethnic Identity: Narratives by Asian American Professionals* (1999)

Wendy Ho, *In Her Mother's House: The Politics of Asian American Mother–Daughter Writing* (2000)

Deborah Woo, *Glass Ceilings and Asian Americans: The New Face of Workplace Barriers* (2000)

Patricia Wong Hall and Victor M. Hwang, editors, *Anti-Asian Violence in North America: Asian American and Asian Canadian Reflections on Hate, Healing, and Resistance* (2001)

Pyong Gap Min and Jung Ha Kim, editors, *Religions in Asian America: Building Faith Communities* (2001)

Submission Guidelines

Prospective authors of singly authored or coauthored books and editors of anthologies should submit a letter of introduction, the manuscript or a four- to ten-page proposal, a book outline, and a curriculum vitae to:

Critical Perspectives on Asian Pacific Americans Series
AltaMira Press
1630 North Main Street, #367
Walnut Creek, CA 94596

Anti-Asian Violence in North America

Asian American and Asian Canadian Reflections on Hate, Healing, and Resistance

EDITED BY
PATRICIA WONG HALL AND VICTOR M. HWANG

ALTAMIRA
PRESS

A Division of
ROWMAN & LITTLEFIELD PUBLISHERS, INC.
Walnut Creek • Lanham • New York • Oxford

AltaMira Press
A Division of Rowman & Littlefield Publishers, Inc.
1630 North Main Street, #367
Walnut Creek, CA 94596
http://www.altamirapress.com

Rowman & Littlefield Publishers, Inc.
4720 Boston Way
Lanham, MD 20706

12 Hid's Copse Road
Cumnor Hill, Oxford OX2 9JJ, England

Copyright © 2001 by AltaMira Press

British Library Cataloguing in Publication Information Available

Library of Congress Cataloging-in-Publication Data

Anti-Asian violence in North America : Asian American and Asian Canadian reflections
on hate, healing, and resistance / edited by Patricia Wong Hall and Victor M. Hwang.
    p. cm. — (Critical perspectives on Asian Pacific Americans series)
Includes bibliographical references and index.
ISBN 0-7425-0458-1 (cloth : alk. paper) — ISBN 0-7425-0459-X (pbk. : alk. paper)
    1. Asian Americans—Crimes against. 2. Asians—Crimes against—Canada. 3. Hate
crimes—United States. 4. Hate crimes—Canada. I. Hall, Patricia Wong, 1951– II. Hwang,
Victor M., 1967– III. Series.

HV6250.5.E75 A57 2001
364.1—dc21   00-056931

Printed in the United States of America

⊗™ The paper used in this publication meets the minimum requirements of
American National Standard for Information Sciences—Permanence of Paper for
Printed Library Materials, ANSI/NISO Z39.48–1992.

*This book is dedicated to our parents,
to our families,
and to the past victims of hate crimes.*

Contents

Part Two: Language and Identity

Part Three: Growth and Resistance

Part Four: Epilogue and Afterword

Acknowledgments

We would like to thank the following people for their help with this manuscript on anti-Asian violence in North America:

In Canada, to Messrs. Kenda Gee, Jim Wong Chu, Sandy Yep, Michael Denyszyn, Terry Watada, Andy Yan, and Bernard Nguyen The Mai, for their help and knowledge of Asian Canadian history and literature.

In the United States, our thanks to Dr. Bruce Sullivan for his computer expertise and assistance.

We are grateful to our families and friends who have helped us with their words of encouragement and support.

Our thanks to the Asian Law Caucus of San Francisco, California.

Thank you to Jennifer Collier and the staff at AltaMira Press for their support and encouragement throughout this process.

As project editor, Patricia Hall, would like to especially thank Victor Hwang for all of his help with this book manuscript and the seemingly endless stream of emails that finally resulted in the publication of this volume.

Finally, a special thank you to all of the contributors in this volume for their collective efforts and hard work.

Patricia Wong Hall
Victor M. Hwang

Introduction

P. W. Hall

The hottest places in hell are reserved for those who, in times of great moral crisis, maintain their neutrality.

Dante (1265–1321)

I began working on the project to produce a volume on anti-Asian violence in 1992, in an effort to educate the public about hate crimes. After connecting with a group of Asian Canadians a few years ago at a writers' conference in Vancouver, I decided to include in this hate-crimes book the perspectives and personal reflections of Asian Canadians and Asian Americans.

The essays come from a social, psychological, or historical perspective on hate crimes. This collection is extraordinary—none other like it currently exists—and it represents the state of the art in the field of studying anti-Asian violence. For the first time, the voices of Asian Americans and Asian Canadians have been brought together in one volume to discuss hate crimes and racial hatred in their lives. The collective history of these two groups of people gives testimony as to why such a collection is needed.

The writers themselves come from diverse backgrounds and cover a wide range of occupational backgrounds; they include several attorneys, a teacher, community activists, graduate students, and professionals. Because hate crimes span legal, social, and emotional contexts, many of the contributors have chosen a narrative style that blends theory, social commentary, and personal experience. In this way, each writer is able to move between contextual and individual issues that range from ethnic identity and personal growth to institutionalized racism and legal structures. Many of the essays discuss the legacy of distrust embedded in racism. From stories that span issues of immigration to civil rights, gender and identity to Internet violence and community resistance, a number of important themes emerge. After reviewing these, I will offer some historical background with which to contextualize contemporary episodes of hate crimes against people of Asian descent.

THEMES IN ANTI-ASIAN VIOLENCE

Michelle Yoshida begins the volume with a narrative that sets the stage for understanding the relationship between the individual and the social aspects of hate crimes. A former special assistant to a commissioner of the U.S. Commission on Civil Rights, she uses a personal story of a threat against her own life to make broad observations about civil rights and the process of pursuing justice against perpetrators of hate crimes. Her story weaves through the tribulations of her court case, defining the federal statue on hate crimes (Title 18 of the U.S. Code, Section 245(b)) and describing her work with a coalition of lawyers to pass the federal 1999 Hate Crimes Prevention Act, which was thwarted by Congress in 1999. Yoshida's lucid and riveting account of her case reveals the effect it had not only on her own life, but also on the lives of many, and often unrecognized, victims of hate crimes. As she has observed, every hate crime affects not only the targeted victim, but the targeted community as well. Thus, Yoshida applies the doctrine of "transferred intent" to the hate-crime arena, showing how the effects of the original hate crime are transferred from the targeted victim to others who also suffer the consequences of illegal acts driven by bigotry, intolerance, and ignorance. This argument reveals the limitations of the federal hate-crime statutes and the need for stronger federal hate-crime legislation.

Victor Hwang, coeditor of this volume, extends this discussion about the role of the victim in hate crimes within the context of

Asian Pacific American communities, linking social and legal contexts to the development of collective community identity. Hwang himself describes his contribution as discussing

> the role of anti-Asian violence as a foil and as a catalyst in the development of an Asian American identity and a community. Our community lives in the contradiction, in the friction between competing notions of ethnicity and nationality, in the margins and as a wedge between Black and White in American society. It is not a physical community, but one that exists in flashes, in movements, in speeches, in hearts and minds, and in struggle. It is within the heat of the response to these incidents of extreme racial violence that we continue to forge our identity and our sense of community.

Hwang's paper, he points out, "discusses the formation of community by dissecting two recent incidents of anti-Asian violence and the subsequent responses."

In addition to physical incidents, language and speech are particularly important in the mobilization and development of the communities and ethnic identities that Hwang describes. Ashok Mathur's important contribution looks at the connection between language and violence. He uses "counter-storytelling," one of the basic tenets of critical race theory, to articulate how language can and does function as an oppressive tool that contributes to the perpetuation of hate. "By reflecting on storytelling episodes where racialization and racial epithets figure prominently," Mathur reflects, "the article suggests that hateful speech has pernicious power and the ability to regulate the constructions of racial (and other forms of) identity. The central argument is that words and language, while perhaps not so overt as boots and fists, are most certainly acts of hate that help to maintain oppressive power structures." The stories he tells in his chapter are "about a form of violence, about how language and its components can comprise a type of sustained, systematic assault." The relationship between words and violence is reflected in essays throughout this book: words can create violent riots or build powerful coalitions of resistance. In the very writing of these chapters, the authors in this volume are enacting Mathur's assertion that resistance occurs in the telling and retelling of these stories.

An attorney, college instructor, and activist, Eric Mar inspires such retellings in his courses on Asian American studies and ethnic studies. In his chapter, from his front-line activism in the San Francisco Bay Area since the 1980s, he recounts the history of the prominent Kao and Vincent Chin cases, and of the death of George Lee, a leader of the tenants'-justice and social-justice movements in San Francisco. Out of these cases has emerged a rainbow coalition against police brutality. Mar's students and the new generations of activists continually renew his hope for the future of justice movements for Asian Americans. Mr. Mar thoroughly examines the Kao and Chin cases. As with most hate crimes, both Asian American men were dehumanized by their perpetrators and died tragically and violently.

In the twenty-first century, technology is engendering new kinds of ethnic communities. In "Hate Crime on the Internet: The University of California, Irvine, Case," Mavis Lee examines the crime, the investigation, and the trial that ultimately resulted in the first successful prosecution of a hate crime on the Internet. She discusses the reactions and responses from some of the Asian and Asian American students at UCI to being the target of a hate crime, and the negative effects the hate e-mail had on them. She also discusses the approach used by the defense attorney in the case, the reactions of some of the jurors, and the reactions of Mr. Machado, the perpetrator, to his actions.

Other unique features of many Asian American communities are their international and cross-cultural ties, and their extensive immigrant populations. Misa Joo's relationship to a Laotian family in Oregon shows that the personal and social or cultural dimensions of hate crimes can be particularly complex for new immigrants. Joo writes about helping her Laotian friends cope—legally, emotionally, and psychologically—with the rape and murder of their daughter in a new country, with new cultural, judicial, and community rules. The family had to cope with the fact that this crime would likely not have happened in Laos, and it bears a profound effect on the trajectory of their lives in the United States.

One aspect of the immigrant experience, and certainly of any ethnic community that is the object of hate crimes, is the differential treatment immigrants receive from public and legal institutions. Terry Watada extends the connections established between individual and social racism in an essay on a series of hate-crime charges brought against the Toronto police department in the 1990s. In a majority of these cases, the charges against the police have been dropped. Watada asks the fundamental question: whom do the Canadian police protect and serve? If the police are committing, rather than preventing, hate crimes in Canada, are they no better than the skinheads? In this case, hate crimes are something that set Asian Canadian communities outside of the citizen constituency of the public police force. Watada has this to say about his essay:

> I don't trust cops and with good reason. As a kid, I was once threatened at gunpoint by a police detective. He lived on my street and played with us like he was one of the gang. But he harbored an unfathomable hatred for me. Lately, there has been a disturbing trend in Toronto, Canada. The police have been using deadly force as a first response when dealing with citizens of color. The burning question at issue is why is the first response the last response in these cases? Is racism at the core of these actions? "To Serve and Protect" examines my responses to hate crimes perpetrated by the police as an outgrowth of the lessons I learned as a child at the end of a gun barrel.

Doug A. Tang and Jia Ling both draw from their understandings of the social contexts of racism and hate crimes to write more personal narratives on the development of ethnic and gender identity. Growing up in Texas, Doug A. Tang struggled with racism, psychosis, and masculinity. In his life, the three phenomena have combined in ways that have tested both his dignity as a male and his mental integrity. Mr. Tang says that he is torn between his beliefs in nonviolence, Gandhi, and Martin Luther King, and his desire to harm his harassers. Tang covers various topics in his essay: masculinity and Asian Pacific American men; stereotypes of Asians and Asian Americans in Hollywood; Asian Americans and self-loathing; self-genocide and counseling; and the idea that Asian Americans have been and are still viewed as rats or dogs to some mainstream Americans. Tang asserts that Asian Americans must stop the self-hate and embrace their race and their communities, in spite of anti-Asian violence. He relates his experiences to the larger struggles of Asian Americans to define and prove themselves as men and women. His essay is a powerful statement on the psychological ramifications of hate crimes on people of Asian descent in America.

Jia Ling also turns inward to consider the personal and developmental impacts of racism and hatred in "Am I Beautiful Now?" Exploring the intersections of beauty, gender, and ethnicity for Asian Americans, her insightful essay examines the sometimes painful depths of being female and Asian American for some women in the United States. When an individual grows up in the context of external and social racism, the result can be self-hatred and self-destruction. Ling discusses her own fight against internal and external hate and silence, and she addresses her resistance and the strength she developed both individually and in the context of Asian American communities.

Ritz Chow, also writing about immigration, develops the discussion of silence as itself a form of resistance against racism, capitalism, homophobia, and other issues. In her theoretical narrative, she draws on her family's experience as Chinese immigrants to Canada, and on the writings of other people of color and other immigrants to the United States and Canada. She weaves a contextual web of multinational economies, cultural differences, and homophobia within which victims of hate must mobilize both individual and collective resistance. Voice and silence are two sides of this coin: in addition to speaking out and fighting against racist violence, she says, "[W]e must also conserve energy to create, to love, to think and reflect, and to survive." This balance also raises generational issues for immigrants undergoing rapid cultural change that may divide children and parents: "Do I do as my parents did and walk away silently to continue working and living? Or do I confront violence, speak out and meet my perpetrators measure for measure? Perhaps the answer lies somewhere in between, where strategies past (parents) and present (me) come to the fore." Both Ling and Chow explore the topic of lesbianism from Asian American and Asian Canadian perspectives, respectively.

A BRIEF HISTORY OF ANTI-ASIAN VIOLENCE

Anti-Asian violence is a topic that has concerned the Asian American and Asian Canadian communities in North America for over a century—indeed, since our ancestors began immigrating to the Americas in the 1800s and early 1900s. Michael and Judy Newton, in *Racial and Religious Violence in America: A Chronology*, state that the first anti-Chinese incident in the United States occurred in 1871 in Colorado, where a Chinese man's home was burned by vandals (212). In two nations dominated by immigrants, Asian Americans and Asian Canadians have nevertheless been treated as perpetual foreigners within their homelands. We have been called "Chinks," "Japs," and other racial slurs for years. It is important to note that the hate crimes we know today have their roots in both legally sanctioned and illegal behavior.

Legislation against Asian immigrants was first enacted in the United States in the 1880s with the first federal exclusion acts. At that point, Asian immigrants were primarily Chinese American men who worked the gold mines or on U.S. railroads for lower wages than Whites and took the unwanted jobs. They were sojourners with dreams of returning to China or bringing their families to America to reunite with them. In spite of their unique contributions to the U.S. economy, recessions have inspired riots against them since the 1800s.

DEFINING AND COUNTING HATE CRIMES IN THE UNITED STATES

Today, multiple definitions exist for hate crimes. Jenness and Grattet in an article for *Sociological Perspectives* relate the definition used by the Hate Crimes Statistics Act of 1990 that calls them "crimes in which the defendant's conduct was motivated by hatred, bias, or prejudice based on the actual or perceived race, color, religion, national origin, ethnicity, gender, or sexual orientation of another individual or group of individuals" (U.S. Congress 1992). Jacobs and Henry define hate crimes as "crimes against persons or property motivated in whole or in part by racial, ethnic, religious, gender, sexual orientation, and other prejudices" (366). According to the National Asian Pacific American Legal Consortium, the FBI (Federal Bureau of Investigation) defines a hate crime as "any criminal act that is motivated by the victim's actual or perceived race, ethnicity, religion, sexual orientation, disability or gender." Finally, the Anti-Defamation League defines a hate crime as "an act or an attempted act by any person against the person or property of another individual or group which in any way constitutes an expression of hostility toward the victim because of the victim's actual or perceived race, religion, sexual orientation, national origin, disability, gender or ethnicity."

My coeditor, Victor Hwang, also an attorney with the Asian Law Caucus in San Francisco, offers some perspective on the myriad definitions and contexts of hate crimes:

> There's not really a difference between the legal standard for hate crimes for the purposes of gathering stats and those for criminal law. *It's just a matter of how high a burden of proof you use.* For statistics purposes, we use a lower threshold—if we think it's a hate-motivated incident, we count it. For law enforcement, it's proof beyond a reasonable doubt like all other criminal cases. The bigger standard is in the use of the terms "anti-Asian violence" (AAV) and "hate crime." [For it] to be a hate crime, you must have a crime, meaning that someone must commit a vandalism, battery, murder, assault, threat . . . and be substantially motivated by racial prejudice. The term AAV is broader and encompasses things like being called a "Chink" or "Jap" without a clear threat of violence—which would be covered under the First Amendment and therefore not a crime, but could be called an incident of AAV.

Hwang gives as an example a 1998 case in Fremont, California:

> Two white men in a pickup truck rolled up to a South Asian elderly woman dressed in traditional garb (an Indian sari) and threw a bucket of feces at her. The cops refused to consider this a hate crime because of the lack of evidence (the two men did not say anything). We think that due to lack of economic motivation . . . and given the recent history of racial tensions in Fremont—it's a hate crime. (E-mail, December 28, 1999)

This case, along with most of the essays in this volume, demonstrates that there is vast disagreement about what constitutes a hate crime. The variability and quantity of factors to consider in any given case make formal and legal definitions difficult. How does any organization, activist, or individual proceed to count, understand, or fight such phenomena?

Hwang's organization, the National Asian Pacific American Legal Consortium (NAPALC), is one organization that tackles these issues head on. NAPALC is a nonprofit agency designed to protect the legal and civil rights of Asian Pacific Americans (APAs) through litigation, public education, and other means. With headquarters in Washington, D.C., it is comprised of the Asian American Legal Defense and Education Fund in New York, the Asian Law Caucus in San Francisco, and the Asian Pacific American Legal Center of Southern California in Los Angeles. With such a broad presence, the organization is able to collect data and initiate activism on a national scale.

The consortium reported that in 1996, the FBI recorded nearly eighty-six hundred hate crimes in the United States. The consortium's *1997 Audit of Violence against Asian Pacific Americans—Fifth Annual Report* states that anti-Asian violence has increased sharply in the United States since 1995. A 1997 FBI report showed that forty states have legislation that addresses hate crimes due to race, religion, or ethnicity. Eleven states did not collect hate-crime statistics in 1997. Among the outstanding cases from 1997, the list includes *Lizardo v. Denny's, Inc.* (from New York), *Truong v. San Francisco Housing Authority*, and the *U.S. v. Machado* (the UC Irvine Internet case).

In NAPALC's *1998 Audit of Violence against Asian Pacific Americans*, a chart of anti-Asian incidents by the ethnicity of victims indicated the following percentages: Chinese: 25 percent; Vietnamese: 16 percent; Korean: 10 percent; Japanese: 9 percent; South Asian: 32 percent; Filipino: 5 percent; Thai/Lao/multiracial: 1 percent; and Samoan: 2 percent (14). The 1998 consortium also gave a synopsis of the most notable hate-crimes cases to 1999 against Asian Americans. And an article titled "A Ten-Year Retrospective of Anti-Asian Hate Violence," by Sin Yen Ling of the Asian American Legal Defense and Education Fund, lists the names, descriptions, locations, and years for hate crimes against people of Asian descent in the United States for 1998. In 1999, these sources report, Asian hate-crime victims included Joseph Ileto (California), Naoki Kamijima (Illinois), and Won Joon Yoon (Indiana). In 1998, the most memorable American victims were Rishi Maharaj (New York), Loi Nguyen (Phoenix), the Patels (Maryland), and a group of South Asian men (California). According to an article by Jason Ma in *Asian Week*, a Korean American named John Lee suffered a cracked skull in a hate crime at the State University of New York-Binghamton in February 2000. These are merely a few representational cases of crimes that occur in neighborhoods, schools, homes, and public and private settings of every kind. By any definition, hate crimes are a critical and frightening reality.

ASIAN AMERICAN WOMEN

According to the FBI's Uniform Crime Report, 8,759 hate crimes were documented in the United States in 1996 alone (Anti-Defamation League 3). The report further states that 63 percent of those hate crimes were motivated by race, 14 percent by religion, 12 percent by sexual orientation, and 11 percent by ethnicity. As with hate crimes as a whole, such further subcategories are difficult distinctions to make. The ADL (Anti-Defamation League) contends that "gender-based hate crimes cannot be easily distinguished from other forms of hate-motivated violence," and the narratives in this book bring the point home. The ADL further states that there have not occurred an "overwhelming number of gender-based crimes reported as an extension of domestic violence and rape cases" (Anti-Defamation League 3). The ADL added gender to its model hate-crimes statute in 1996. Federal protections include the Hate Crimes Sentencing Act, the Church Arsons Prevention Act, the Hate Crimes Statistics Act, and the Violence against Women Act of 1994.

A pending Hate Crimes Prevention Act would equalize the variety of protections offered to women by state laws. This act would allow federal officials to investigate and prosecute cases where bias violence occurred and would, according to the ADL, allow "federal prosecution without requiring proof that the victim was attacked because he or she was engaged in an activity protected under the [American] Bill of Rights." However, the track record shows that gender- and race-based violence often escape prosecution (Anti-Defamation League 3). This is a problem that needs to be closely monitored. Civil rights movements, traditionally strong on asserting race and ethnic rights, must be equally attuned to dimensions of gender inequality. Activists must reexamine prevailing views on gender-based violence against women of color.

According to Helen Zia:

> The anti-Asian violence movement, like the criminal justice establishment, doesn't consider violence against women "hate crimes.". . . Initially, there was a lot of resistance within the anti-Asian violence movement, which said that gender crimes are one thing and hate crimes another. . . .When a woman of color or Asian woman is sexually assaulted, is she being targeted for being a women or for being Asian? At what point does the anti-Asian violence movement pick it up? . . . Now there is a federal Violence against Women Act, which describes gender-motivated crimes as hate crimes. (Chiang 1997, 64)

In America, the National Organization of Women (NOW) has urged Congress to amend Section 245 of Title 18 of the U.S. Criminal Code for "the inclusion of sexual orientation and gender bias crimes to the number of bias-motivated crimes that can be investigated and penalized by the government. This move has been prompted by the increase of offenses motivated by a person's real or perceived sex or sexual orientation," according to the *National N.O.W. Times* in 1997.

ASIAN CANADIAN HATE CRIMES

The history of violence against people of Asian descent in Canada runs parallel to the history in the United States, and mutual influences have existed between official and unofficial anti-Asian sentiment in both countries. Bernard Nguyen The Mai and Terry Watada believe that the first Chinese arrived in

1788 as part of an expedition with Captain John Meares in Victoria Island, British Columbia (e-mail from Bernard Nguyen The Mai, May 21, 1999). However, the first substantial wave of Asian immigrants came to Canada in 1858 during the gold rush. Mai traces the first Chinese back to Chang Tsoo and Ah Hong, who immigrated to Victoria in 1858 to search for gold in the Fraser River. Race riots began around 1877; a similar riot in 1871 in the United States left twenty-three Chinese men dead in Los Angeles. According to Mr. Kenda Gee, founder of Edmonton's Asian Heritage Month (e-mail, July 7, 1999), head taxes on Asians were enforced in Canadian provinces, with the first federal head tax occurring in 1885 for fifty dollars. By 1903, the amount rose to five hundred dollars. The first British Canadian exclusion laws came in 1907, shortly after similar laws were enacted in the United States. Also in 1907, the Asiatic Expulsion League organized an anti-Asian riot—a copycat of the 1907 riot in Bellingham, Washington.

In 1908, a federal immigration law denied the immigration of non-Whites. The total exclusion of the Chinese came with the 1923 Chinese Immigration Act, just three years after the foundation of the Ku Klux Klan in Canada. The act was finally repealed in 1947 when the Chinese were given the right to vote. Between 1942 and 1949, however, Japanese Canadians were deported and interned just as they were in the United States. And as in the United States, Japanese Canadians campaigned until they won a redress agreement in 1988.

Today, the legacy of anti-Asian racism remains. Unfortunately, there exists no national survey of anti-Asian violence in Canada, and statistics are available only for each province. This is in contrast to current methods of tracking hate crimes nationally in the United States. Sandy Yep and Michael Denyszyn of the Canadian Race Relations Foundation (CRRF) have been working closely with the Ottawa-Carleton Regional Police Service, which has uncovered the following statistics on anti-Asian violence in Ottawa, Canada: thirteen cases were reported in 1998; nine in 1997; twenty-five in 1996; and ten in 1995 (e-mail from Sandy Yep, May 21, 1999).

According to Ritz Chow (from this volume), a trial was held in British Columbia a few years ago for a young White woman who was convicted for the murder of a young South Asian woman named Reena Virk. More recently, a young South Asian male jumped to his death after being harassed at his high school for being "different" (e-mail, May 10, 2000).

TORONTO, CANADA

The Hate Crime Unit Intelligence Services (a division of the Metro Toronto Police Service) has been publishing hate-crime statistics since 1993 based on offenses reported to the Metro Toronto Police Service. The unit's 1998 report defines a "hate crime" as "a criminal offence committed against a person or property that is based upon the victim's race, national or ethnic origin, language, colour, religion, sex, age, mental or physical disability, sexual orientation, or any other similar factor" (Metro Toronto Police Service 1). In the same report, the unit reported that 6 percent of the hate crimes that had occurred in Toronto since 1993 were anti-Asian. By comparison, 28 percent were anti-Black, 15 percent were anti-Semitic, and 7 percent were anti-gay. It also reported that assault was the most common hate-crime offense committed by males between twelve and twenty-five years of age. In 1997, most hate crimes were committed in July, on Thursdays and Sundays. And according to the report, hate crimes occurred most often (in descending order) in (1) public places, (2) residences, (3) education centers, and (4) places of employment. In 1997, fifty-seven arrests were made for hate crimes. That same year, 187 hate crimes were reported, a 7 percent increase over 1996.

In response to this increase, the Hate Crime Unit has focused on education, prevention, and criminal investigations, and has provided hate-bias training to 390 crown attorneys. Other teaching methods have included hate-bias training for officers, detectives, and civilians, and hate-crimes lectures to schools and youth. These are important steps, but the statistics—and experiences like those Watada writes about in this volume—show that police forces and communities have a long way to go.

ASIAN CANADIAN WOMEN

In Canada, as in the United States, intersections of gender and race in the national culture and economy create particularly complex threats of violence against women of color. The Canadian Panel on Violence against Women has articulated the systemic nature of these intersections in Canadian society:

> [I]deologies, policies, and social practices are rooted in the idea that "whites have the right to dominate (non-whites)." Canadians are generally presumed to be white and this is the central reference point of all social institutions. Therefore, racism is structural in nature and cannot be explained as the product of bad communication among individuals. . . . Racism, like sexism, is an integral part of the political and economic system under which we live. . . . Race, gender, and class issues intersect in the labor market. Women are seen as a secondary source of labor. Racist ideologies which "justify" low wages for non-white women force them into bad working conditions. Women of color are triply oppressed due to their race, gender, and class, which compounds their social inequality. Women of color who experience violence suffer from having both their gender and race attacked. When she calls on systems to help, she cannot trust that those systems will value or understand her experience as a non-white female. (19–20)

The issues raised by the panel can be applied to women of color all over the world who are dealing with issues of domestic violence or rape. Clearly, women also have more difficulty seeking redress from social systems such as the law, government, or even health care. The panel has taken the initial steps of recommending a series of national and personal action plans to combat or help alleviate the situation for non-White women.

THE IMPACT OF HATE CRIMES ON GAY VICTIMS

Gregory M. Herek has discussed the findings of his research among gay and lesbian hate-crime victims in his article "The Impact of Hate Crime Victimization," coauthored with J. Cogan and R. J. Gillis. His principal findings are that these survivors of hate crimes experienced longer periods of stress, depression, and anger—a "heightened sense of personal danger and vulnerability that becomes associated with their identity as a gay man or lesbian." Because of homophobia, they perceive the world to be "more dangerous, unpredictable, and hostile," and that the negative effects of hate crimes may last "as long as five years after the victimization occurred" (5). These views are reflected in Jia Ling's essay in this volume.

Certainly, some of these negative-impact statements from gays and lesbians can also be applied to Asian Americans, Asian Canadians, and others who have experienced anti-Asian violence. Hate crimes have the effect of taking away the identity, dignity, and humanity of their victims, regardless of race, nationality, sexual preference, gender, or religion. Depression, stress, and anger are common reactions to and are the natural outcomes of racial violence. Like gays and lesbians, victims of racial hate crimes may well perceive the world as "more dangerous." Recovery times for victims will vary according to the individuals involved in each of the hate crimes. People have different rates of healing and different lengths of time required to process negative stimuli. Nevertheless, it is important to recognize the additional level of stigmatization experienced by gays and lesbians. Social services, juries, judges, and laws are often both ignorant of their needs and biased against or openly hostile to their sexuality.

THE INTERNET AND HATE GROUPS

How is racism being spread throughout North America and the world in the twenty-first century? According to Dan Corrigan, racist flyers were distributed by White supremacists in St. Louis, Missouri, in 1998, proclaiming the near-extinction of the White race due to interracial dating and speaking of the goal by 2004 of zero tolerance. Leafleting parking lots has been one way for racists to get their hate literature to the public. In fact, the ADL reports that shopping malls in the Missouri/Southern Illinois area were leafleted in this fashion, with material from the "14 Word Press," an Internet homepage that features hate sites, including those of the Volksfront, Stormfront, Ku Klux Klan, Women for Aryan Unity, White Aryan Resistance, and White Power World Wide (Anti-Defamation League 3). Corrigan states that many of these hate groups have utilized the Internet to spread their campaigns of hatred to millions.

In the August/September 1999 issue of *Ms.* magazine, Ariel Gore reported that more than 1,400 hate groups had sites on the Internet. The winter 2000 issue of *The Intelligence Report* listed a total of 305 hate sites on the World Wide Web. The Southern Poverty Law Center, ADL, NAPALC, and other groups represent a significant force in monitoring such hate groups and their activities.

On March 2, 2000, in a story titled "Road to Hate" featured on the television program *Dateline*, Tom Brokaw reported on Matthew Williams, who is in a Shasta County, California, prison for killing gays and burning synagogues. Williams began using the Internet in 1995, where he connected with various White-supremacist hate groups. Williams, age thirty-one, believes that Asians and Blacks have no souls and are not human, and he advocates an "American Dream" of a pure, White society. If these proliferating reports are any indication, new technologies are being utilized effectively to spread racial and ethnic hate, and we must in turn direct the attention of our resistance to these new media.

REASONS FOR ANTI-ASIAN VIOLENCE

A 1999 *Jet* magazine article stated that racial prejudice motivated 60 percent of the 8,049 hate crimes reported to the FBI in 1997. Many scholars, such as Jenness and Broad in *Hate Crimes: New Social Movements and the Politics of Violence*, see the connections between social problems and victimization (5). Others, such as Green, Glaser, and Rich, and Lee and Bankston, have found connections between socioeconomics and hate crimes.

In *Hate Crimes: The Rising Tide of Bigotry and Bloodshed*, Levin and McDevitt argue that hatred has become "hip" and that it is "in" with young adults. The Boston Police Hate Crime Tabulations from the 1980s recorded the most common reasons given for hate crimes: the victim(s) was "passing through a neighborhood," or racism (Levin and McDevitt, 246). All of the personal essays in this volume reflect these phenomena.

The *SPLC Report* (published by the Southern Poverty Law Center) from December 1999 blames the rise in hate crimes on the "growing underclass of white suburban youths" in America. These youths are "products of dysfunctional families" (1). This rise in "socioeconomic discontent" and poverty amongst troubled youth jumped 52 percent between 1975 and 1993 in U.S. lower-middle-class suburbs (3). A number of youths have become drawn into the drug world, especially with the use of amphetamines, and the criminal underworld. In addition, the SPLC states that in the year 2000, California Whites will "become a minority for the first time in over a century—a pattern other states will follow between now and 2050" (3).

Clearly, then, class and economic issues have contributed to hate crimes. Eric Mar's chapter in this volume mentions the case of Vincent Chin, who was bludgeoned to death with a baseball bat in 1982 by two unemployed White auto workers in Detroit. Chin's killers mistook him for a Japanese person and blamed their unemployment on him. Many believe that class issues contributed to Chin's death, in addition to racist hatred, since the perpetrators were unemployed. Mar states that "it wasn't until the early 1980s, after Vincent Chin's killing, that [my] racial and class identity really hit me." Chin's death was a wake-up call for many Asian Americans. According to reporter Eunice Park, in an article in *Asian Week* about Detroit, racism "remains a virulent force" today. In the years ahead, attention needs to refocus on the problem of class disparities, as well as on educating the public to dispel the negative stereotypes of people of Asian heritage. This is especially true for those involved in social and community activism, resistance work, legal work, law enforcement, victim-assistance work, and the like.

In his *Harvard Law Review* article "Racial Violence against Asian Americans," Jerry Kang tells us that "physically, hate crimes are usually more brutal than other crimes" and that "psychologically, they invoke a feeling of helplessness, because race—the only characteristic that could be changed to avoid future attacks—is immutable" (1928). According to Kang, Asian Americans are seen as choice victims because of a number of racial stereotypes: they are seen as members of the merchant class or as rich tourists, they are viewed as physically weak and culturally adverse to defending themselves, and (for Asian immigrants in particular) they are less likely to report crimes to the police (1930). Kang asserts that people of Asian descent are not viewed as equal to the dominant culture and are blamed for the ills of society. Asian Americans are seen by perpetrators as "submissive," as the "model minority," as "unfair competitors" (an unwelcome economic threat), as "foreigners," and "are seen not as individuals, but as fungible" (exchangeable, interchangeable; 1932). In addition, women of Asian descent are sometimes stereotyped as "exotic geishas" or are romanticized by mainstream society, rather than being seen as ordinary human beings. Also, because prostitution has existed during wartime in various parts of Asia, this negative connotation has stigmatized Asian women. In this volume, Jia Ling also addresses these issues.

Kang states that what often results from these negative belief systems is that the "individual becomes hostile towards people of Asian ancestry as a group, then decides to commit violence, and, finally, chooses his victim" (1933). Scapegoating is common because "Asian Americans are blamed as unfair competitors, as the model minority," etc. Perpetrators believe that Asian Americans are unfair competitors because "they consume resources that would otherwise go to 'real' Americans" (1935). Kang's article goes on to by remind us that "history lends insight into this process of dehumanization" (1937).

SOME SOLUTIONS TO HATE CRIMES AND THE FUTURE OF HATE-CRIMES WORK

Many possible solutions to hate crimes exist. Jenness and Broad discuss coalition-building around issues of intolerance (55). Their work deals with the history of violence and with hate crimes as a social problem, and is concerned primarily with gays, lesbians, and women. It is their contention that much is to be learned from the antiviolence movements of the 1960s, such as the civil rights movement, women's movement, and gay/lesbian movement (28). They assert that three kinds of antiviolence movements now exist: (1) citizen action groups (neighborhood watches), (2) victim-services movements (hot lines), and (3) racial-justice movements (against police brutality, such as CAAAV; see below). The central component in these movements is the advocacy of support given to the victims (28), which is recognized as a key element in successful programs.

Kelly and Maghan also discuss ways to deter hate crimes and note that the majority of such crimes are committed by teenagers (167). The authors note that "young people who commit such crimes often have confused and antisocial personalities," and argue for stricter juvenile-justice laws for hate crimes (168). This sort of deviance model, however, should not belittle the fact that racism is mainstream and systemic; as Levin and McDevitt have argued, some youth think that hate is hip. Kelly and Maghan do cite the importance of the symbolic denunciation of hate crimes by our politicians and other public figures to counter the trend of social acceptance of hate crimes.

In *Mass Hate: The Global Rise of Genocide and Terror*, Neil Kressel devotes an entire chapter to the solutions for hate crimes; the chapter tells us why individuals participate in hate crimes and explores ways to fight hate by promoting a world with less mass hatred (247–81). Others, including Nelson Mandela, Martin Luther King Jr., Elie Wiesel, and Mohandas Gandhi, have tried to teach tolerance to the masses. Some, such as the Dalai Lama, believe that tolerance and love are increasing in the world. All of these leaders have used a variety of techniques in an effort to increase world peace. While some believe that law enforcement acts to maintain the peace, many others think that police brutality is increasing in this country (as exemplified by the Rodney King case). The authors in this volume, all in their own ways, explore the difficult contradictions between violence and peace as they develop individual positions through healing and resistance.

The work of community activism and of programs that fight hate crimes is reviewed in *Multicultural Law Enforcement: Strategies for Peacekeeping in a Diverse Society*, where editors Shusta, Levine, Harris, and Wong assert the importance of cultural awareness and diversity training, of hate-crime response strategies, and of the need for this training for police officers. Some of the suggestions given for instructors of cultural-sensitivity training sessions include being empathetic with participants, allowing for controversy, providing for follow-up support groups, and identifying potentially hostile employees (99). The book also covers war-related hate crimes (284), a hate-crime response model policy (290–93), and law-enforcement contact with Asian Pacific Americans, as well as with immigrants.

Herek, Cogan, and Gillis also list some helpful suggestions for prevention work:

> [I]dentify ways in which the threat of hate crime victimization affects the well-being of communities; find ways to improve services to hate crimes victims by training law enforcement personnel, health care professionals, mental health professionals, and social service providers; enact the Hate Crimes Prevention Act of 1998 and support federal anti-discrimination laws, statutes and regulations; increase support of the Community Relations Service of the Department of Justice, which resolves racial conflicts; encourage educational projects in communities to dispel minority stereotypes, reduce racial hostility and encourage intercultural understanding; and encourage law enforcement officials, community leaders, educators, and researchers and policymakers to work together to halt hate crimes. (11)

Rita Chaudhry Sethi reminds us to think historically and systemically. She implores people of Asian heritage to understand "how racism operates socially and institutionally" in their countries against themselves and other people of color. She asserts that people of Asian ancestry need to "acknowledge their own complicity," and that accepting themselves as people of color, they must come to understand their shared history of "being targeted as visibly Other. Only then can we act in solidarity with other efforts at ending racism" (238). As an example, Sethi links current violence to the historical fact that Asians have been a cheap source of labor for the railroads since the early 1800s and have been seen as an economic threat (243). She asks, "When auto workers beat up Vincent Chin, was it Japanese competition in the auto industry or unbridled racism that motivated the murderers?" She answers her own question by stating, "[R]ace and class are inseparable because of the inherent difficulty in identifying the primary or motivating factor; any racial analysis must consider economic scapegoating as an avenue for racial harassment and racial victimization as an excuse for expressing economic tensions" (244).

CONCLUSION

By providing a brief introduction on the history of anti-Asian violence and on the people of Asian descent in North America, I hope to encourage readers to further explore these issues using the essays and sources provided in this volume. All North Americans, regardless of their race, would do service to the next generation by educating themselves on race issues. Rita C. Sethi is correct in telling people of color to "act in solidarity with other efforts at ending racism."

Hate-crimes statistics change continually. Therefore, while using this book in their courses, professors and teachers are encouraged to supply students with the most current data by consulting the organizations listed below. Even though the data change, the voices in this collection give rise to a sentiment that is timeless.

P. W. Hall
May 2000

ANTI-VIOLENCE ORGANIZATIONS AND RESOURCES

Many nonprofit organizations in North America are working to combat racial hatred and intolerance. Below appears a partial list of some of these organizations and their contact information:

United States

Anti-Defamation League
Web site: www.adl.org

Committee Against Anti-Asian Violence
Tel: 212-473-6485
E-mail: caaav@dti.net

The CAAAV in New York City cofounded the New York City Coalition against Police Brutality (CAPB) in 1996, in response to the growing number of cases of police brutality there against people of color.

Facing History and Ourselves National Foundation
Web site: www.facing.org

HateWatch
E-mail: info@hatewatch.org

Healing from Hate Crimes
Web site: www.thecpac.com/anti-hate.html

National Asian Pacific American Legal Consortium
Web site: www.napalc.org

This site lists model conflict-resolution programs and violence-prevention programs as well as a resource list. Find these in the 1997 and 1998 reports.

National Center for Conflict Resolution Education
Tel. (toll free): 800-308-9419

Simon Wiesenthal Center Museum of Tolerance Task Force against Hate
Tel. (toll free): 800-900-9036

Southern Poverty Law Center, including Klanwatch
Tel: 334-264-0286
Web site: www.splcenter.org

Canada

Asian Canadian Online
Web site: www.asian.ca (Kenda Gee, Webmaster)

Canadian Race Relations Foundation (Sandy Yep, Program Officer)
Web site: www.crr.ca

Hate Crime Units in Canada
Web site: www.antiracist.com

National Crime Prevention Centre, Canada
Web site: www.crime-prevention.org

BIBLIOGRAPHY

Books

Canadian Panel on Violence against Women. *Changing the Landscape: Ending Violence—Achieving Equality.* Ottawa, Canada: Minister of Supply and Services, 1993.

Chan, Sucheng. *Asian Americans: An Interpretive History.* New York: Twayne Publishers, 1991.

Chiang, Pamela, Milyoung Cho, Elaine H. Kim, Meizhu Lui, and Helen Zia. "On Asian America, Feminism, and Agenda-making—A Roundtable Discussion" (moderated by Seema Shah). In *Dragon Ladies: Asian American Feminists Breathe Fire*, Sonia Shah, ed. Boston: South End Press, 1997.

Ehrlich, Howard, Barbara Larcom, and Robert Purvis. "The Traumatic Impact of Ethnoviolence." In *The Price We Pay: The Case against Racist Speech, Hate Propaganda, and Pornography*, Lederer and Delgado, eds. New York: Hill and Wang, 1995.

Jenness, Valerie, and Kendal Broad. *Hate Crimes: New Social Movements and the Politics of Violence.* New York: Aldine De Gruyter, 1997.

Kelly, Robert J., and Jess Maghan, eds. *Hate Crime: The Global Politics of Polarization.* Carbondale: Southern Illinois University Press, 1998.

Kressel, Neil J. *Mass Hate: The Global Rise of Genocide and Terror.* New York: Plenum Press, 1996.

Lederer, Laura J., and Richard Delgado, eds. *The Price We Pay: The Case against Racist Speech, Hate Propaganda, and Pornography.* New York: Hill and Wang, 1995.

Levin, Jack, and Jack McDevitt. *Hate Crimes: The Rising Tide of Bigotry and Bloodshed.* New York: Plenum Press, 1993.

Newton, Michael, and Judy A. Newton, eds. *Racial and Religious Violence in America: A Chronology.* New York: Garland Publishing, Inc., 1991.

Sethi, Rita C. "Smells Like Racism: A Plan for Mobilizing against Anti-Asian Bias." In *The State of Asian America: Activism and Resistance in the 1990s*, Karin Aguilar-San Juan, ed. Boston: South End Press, 1994.

Shusta, Robert M., Deena Levine, Philip Harris, and Herbert Wong, eds. *Multicultural Law Enforcement: Strategies for Peacekeeping in a Diverse Society.* Englewood Cliffs, N.J.: Prentice Hall, 1995.

Takaki, Ronald. *Strangers from a Different Shore: A History of Asian Americans.* New York: Penguin Books, 1989.

Walker, Samuel. *Hate Speech: The History of an American Controversy.* Lincoln: University of Nebraska Press, 1994.

P. W. Hall

Zia, Helen. "Where Race and Gender Meet: Racism, Hate Crimes, and Pornography." In *The Price We Pay: The Case against Racist Speech, Hate Propaganda, and Pornography*, Lederer and Delgado, eds. New York: Hill and Wang, 1995.

Personal Correspondence

Chow, Ritz. E-mail to author, May 10, 2000.
Gee, Kenda. E-mail to author, July 7, 1999.
Hwang, Victor. E-mail to author, Dec. 28, 1999.
Nguyen, Bernard The Mai. E-mail to author, May 21, 1999.
Yep, Sandy. E-mail to author, May 21, 1999.

Periodicals, Reports, and Other Sources

Anti-Defamation League. *Action Update: Mid-Year Report, 1999*: 3.
Committee Against Anti-Asian Violence. "Struggles for Justice." *CAAAV Voice: Organizing Asian Communities* 10.2 (Fall 1998): 9.
Corrigan, Dan. "Hate Groups Target St. Louis." *St. Louis Journalism Review* 28.205 (April 1998): 1.
Eisler, Dale. "We Killed This Chick: A Regina Murder Trial Has Racial Undercurrents." *Maclean's*, Dec. 16, 1996: 28.
Gore, Ariel. "Ms.cellaneous." *Ms.*, Aug./Sept. 1999: 13.
Green, Donald P., Jack Glaser, and Andrew Rich. "From Lynching to Gay Bashing: The Elusive Connection between Economic Conditions and Hate Crime." *Journal of Personality and Social Psychology* 75.1 (1998): 82–92.
"Hate Groups on the Internet." *The Intelligence Report* 97 (Winter 2000): 36–39.
Herek, Gregory M., J. Cogan, and R. J. Gillis, eds. "The Impact of Hate Crime Victimization." Paper presented at a congressional briefing cosponsored by the American Psychological Association and the Society for the Psychological Study of Social Issues, November 1997, Washington, D.C. As quoted on the American Psychological Association Web site <www.apa.org/pubinfo/hate> under "Hate Crimes Today: An Age-Old Foe in Modern Dress," 1998 [last accessed Dec. 2000].
Hunter, Maclean. "Hate Ruling: Court Rules That Column by Vancouver Writer Doug Collins Was Not Hate Literature." *Maclean's*, Nov. 24, 1997: 90.
Hunter, Maclean. "Keegstra Sentenced: Alberta Court of Appeal Gives Jim Keegstra Stiffer Sentence for Promoting Hatred against Jews." *Maclean's*, Oct. 7, 1997: 29.

Jacobs, James B., and Jessica S. Henry. "The Social Construction of a Hate Crime Epidemic." *Journal of Criminal Law and Criminology* 86.2 (Winter 1996): 366–91.

Jenness, Valerie, and Ryken Grattet. "The Criminalization of Hate: A Comparison of Structural and Polity Influences on the Passage of 'Bias-Crime' Legislation in the United States." *Sociological Perspectives* 39.1 (Spring 1998): 129.

Kang, Jerry. "Racial Violence against Asian Americans." *Harvard Law Review* 106.8 (June 1993): 1926–43.

Lee, Matthew R., and William B. Bankston. "Political Structure, Economic Inequality, and Homicide: A Cross-National Analysis." *Deviant Behavior* 20.1 (1999): 27–55.

Ma, Jason. "Korean American Suffers Cracked Skull in Hate Crime." *Asian Week* 21.31 (Mar. 30, 2000): 9.

Metro Toronto Police Service. "Intelligence Services Hate Crime Report." Toronto, Canada: Hate Crime Unit of Intelligence Services, Feb. 26, 1998.

National Asian Pacific American Legal Consortium. *1997 Audit of Violence against Asian Pacific Americans—Fifth Annual Report: Continuing the Campaign against Hate Crimes.* Washington, D.C.: NAPALC, 1997.

National Asian Pacific American Legal Consortium. "Chart: Anti-Asian Incidents by Ethnicity of Victims, 1998." In *1998 Audit of Violence against Asian Pacific Americans—Sixth Annual Report: The Need for Increased Commitment to Reporting and Community Education.* Washington, D.C.: NAPALC, 1998, 14.

National Asian Pacific American Legal Consortium. "Guidelines and Criteria Used in Evaluating Anti-Asian Incidents." In *1998 Audit of Violence against Asian Pacific Americans—Sixth Annual Report: The Need for Increased Commitment to Reporting and Community Education.* Washington, D.C.: NAPALC, 1998, 34.

National Asian Pacific American Legal Consortium. "Synopses of Notable Cases in 1998–99." In *1998 Audit of Violence against Asian Pacific Americans—Sixth Annual Report: The Need for Increased Commitment to Reporting and Community Education.* Washington, D.C.: NAPALC, 1998, 25–29.

National Conference of State Legislatures. "The Many Kinds of Hate Crime." *State Legislatures* 25.5 (May 1999): 7.

"NOW Pushes to Increase Hate Crimes Prosecution." *National N.O.W. Times* 29.3 (May 1997): 13.

Park, Eunice. "Detroit: Decay and Hope." *Asian Week* 21.15 (Dec. 2, 1999): 13.

"Race Remains Most Frequent Motive for Hate Crimes: FBI Report." *Jet* 95.12 (Feb. 12, 1999): 39.

Sin Yen Ling. "A Ten-Year Retrospective of Anti-Asian Hate Violence." In *1998 Audit of Violence against Asian Pacific Americans—Sixth Annual Report: The Need for Increased Commitment to Reporting and Community Education*. Washington, D.C.: NAPALC, 1998, 11–24.
Southern Poverty Law Center. "Hate Groups Reach Out to a Troubled Generation." *SPLC Report* 29.4 (Dec. 1999): 22–23.

Television Program

Brokaw, Tom. "Road to Hate." *Dateline*. Mar. 2, 2000.

I

✿

ACTIVISM AND THE LAW

1

❦

Transferred Intent: The Pervasiveness of Hate Crimes

Michelle Yoshida

Brrrinnnng . . .
Alone in my office, on yet another typical Monday morning, when the telephone rings. "Commissioner's office," I respond.

I am an attorney, and in late July 1999 I was working as Special Assistant to a Commissioner of the U.S. Commission on Civil Rights, an independent federal agency that strives to protect the civil rights of all Americans and that operates under the executive branch of government. I am also a fourth-generation Japanese American woman.

The man on the other end of the telephone at first seemed frustrated, but there was an aggressive edge to his voice.

"Why do I have to call Washington, D.C., twice in order to get your telephone number in San Francisco when I'm in San Francisco?" he asked. I apologized for the inconvenience, but he flatly rejected it.

"What's your address?" he demanded.

"May I ask who I'm speaking to?" I asked. Then his tone changed. No matter how I describe it to you, you will never understand how much naked aggression and hatred I heard come through the telephone spoken by the man on the other end.

"A FEDERAL TAXPAYER WHO PAYS YOUR FUCKING SALARY! WHAT'S YOUR ADDRESS?"

Fairly new in my position, and believing that since we were a public federal agency this individual was entitled to the information, I gave him our address. "360 Washington Street, Suite 100, San Francisco, California, 94111."

"Fuck you, cunt," he retorted, and hung up the phone.

I was stunned . . . until I realized that I had just given this man my address. The hatred in his voice was enough to terrify me. I knew he was in San Francisco, and he knew where I was.

I immediately telephoned our main office in Washington, D.C., reported the conversation, and advised them that I would be leaving the office for the remainder of the day and working at another location. Before I left, I told the property manager what had happened. He took me to meet two officers of the Federal Protective Service who were on the premises. The officers told me to return to my office, that one of them would be there momentarily to take a report.

The officer as well as the Commissioner arrived at my office, and as I was explaining the situation, the telephone rang again.

I picked up the phone—and immediately recognized the man's voice on the other end.

"Is this the Commission that's supposed to protect our civil rights?" he asked sarcastically. I told him that it was and motioned for the officer to pick up the other telephone and listen in. "If that's true," he continued, "why didn't the Commissioner make a report when [San Francisco Supervisor] Mabel Teng was talking about White boys a few years ago?"

"I don't know," I meekly responded.

"Why not?!" he demanded.

"I don't know."

"I want to speak with the Commissioner," he said.

"I'm sorry, she's in a meeting right now, but if you leave your name and number, I'll ask her to return your call as soon as she can," I offered.

"Why would I want to leave it with a bureaucrat?" his sarcasm continued.

I again made the offer for him to give me his information, and he responded the same.

He then asked when the Commissioner would be back in the office. I said I didn't know.

"You tell the Commissioner that I'm going to slit her fucking throat. Fuck you, bitch." And he hung up on me a second time.

I was terrified now and began to cry out of sheer fear and utter amazement. How was it that someone who knew nothing about me and nothing about the Commissioner could feel enough hatred to call me and make vivid, violent threats?

I composed myself the best that I could and finished telling my story to the officer and the Commissioner. The officer took a report, and we all decided that it would be best if the Commissioner joined me in leaving the office to work at a different location for the remainder of the day. I went to my former law office, and throughout the day I checked my voice mail at the Commission office. In the late afternoon, the same caller left a message: "Yes, I'm interested in dealing with the U.S. Commission on Civil Rights. Why don't you answer your phone? . . . I mean, there's more than just Chinese people in this country, and if you think you're going to impose yourself because of your slant-eyed, yellow asses. . . . I have your address—you better watch your step."

It all made sense now. A week prior to the telephone calls, hate flyers had been distributed to businesses within San Francisco's Chinatown. The flyers were against the Chinese and stated in part:

> We are being ripped off by these sneaky little yellow fuckers and we can't do a damn thing about it. . . . THIS HAS GOT TO STOP. . . . DEMAND THAT THE [sic] SPEAK ENGLISH. . . . DEMAND THAT THEY EITHER GET A GREEN CARD OR GO BACK FROM WHERE EVER [sic] THEY CRAWLED OUT OF. DO YOU REALLY THINK THEY GIVE A SHIT ABOUT US AMERICANS. I CAN TELL YOU, THEY DON'T. . . . STOP THE YELLOW SCUM DO SOMETHING TODAY FOR US WHITE PEOPLE, . . . SPIT ON THEM, FLIP THEM OFF, ANYTHING, BUT DO SOMETHING. THINK ABOUT IT. PUT YOUR BOOT WHERE IT COUNTS. GET THEM FIRST AND GET THEM GOOD!

In response, I had authored an opinion piece under the Commissioner's name deriding the incident and calling on the San Francisco community to stand up to hatred and hate crimes whenever and wherever they occurred. The piece had been published the day prior to the phone calls, in the July 25 Sunday *San Francisco Examiner*.

This man, this caller, had read the opinion piece, and he not only disagreed with it, but he had become virulently proactive—calling Washington, D.C., calling San Francisco, and now making death threats.

LIFE CHANGES

From this point on, my life changed dramatically. I worked at a different location every day, and I received officer escorts whenever I went to the office building to pick up my mail. I had the San Francisco Police Department patrolling my apartment two times a night. I spent every night at a friend's house, because I feared being alone.

My friends noticed the change right away. I became paranoid and anxious. I watched everything and everyone, and I was constantly in a state of high adrenaline whenever I was outside of my home.

Although the Commissioner and not I was the target of the threats, I grew more frightened than I can ever remember being in my life. My attorney friends dubbed me the "transferred-intent victim" because I was not the intended target of the perpetrator, but rather the victim of the fallout. I was the one who had answered the calls and spoken to this man, receiving all of his hatred and taking in his threat to slit the Commissioner's throat.

I also felt extremely guilty. As the author of the published opinion piece, I began to believe that I had "asked for it." That I had brought on this man's hatred and bigotry. That it was my fault.

It took me weeks and an immense amount of support from my friends to realize that it wasn't my fault. I hadn't "asked for" anything. I had done what I thought was right, and I had just caught the attention of someone who was ignorant and bigoted—and proactive. That's where my fear gripped me. Unfortunately, there are ignorant and racist people everywhere, but the ones who go forward and act upon their hate—those are the ones you have to be mindful of. But I also had to realize that this man was not entirely sane and there was nothing I could have done to prepare myself for this. Nor, when I look back on it now, *would* I have done anything differently.

THE INVESTIGATION

After I arrived at my satellite office on July 26, I contacted the San Francisco Police Department's Hate Crimes Unit, reported the incident, and sent them copies of every related document. They opened an investigation.

I also contacted the acting editor of the *San Francisco Examiner's* editorial page to alert him that we had received a threatening response from the published piece. He stated that he and the editorial-pages editor both had received telephone calls from a male caller questioning the legitimacy and authenticity of the opinion piece and demanding to know the telephone number and address of the author. No one at his office had provided the caller with our contact information.

Three days after the telephone calls, an officer joined me to pick up my office mail. I found an envelope bearing scrawled handwriting and no return address. I gave it to the officer and asked him to open it. He examined it, opened it safely, and handed it to me to read.

After reading the first few lines, I knew the letter's author was my threatening caller. I handed it back to the officer and told him that he could keep it. The letter was dated July 25, 1999, and addressed to "Letters to the Editor, San Francisco Examiner." The first line made it clear that the letter was in response to the Commissioner's published opinion piece. In the body of the letter were the exact words he'd spoken to me during the second call, regarding the San Francisco supervisor and her use of the term "White boys." The letter ended "Sincerely," with no signature or further identification.

After I was escorted back to my satellite office, I contacted the *San Francisco Examiner* and faxed them a copy of the letter our office had received. The acting editorial-pages editor said he did not think they had received any written response but he would look into it. I asked that he notify me if he found the original letter with any identifying information, because the federal authorities were eager to speak with the author.

Later that afternoon, I received a voice-mail message from the *Examiner* stating that they had found the original letter with an identification and an address. Apparently, although the threatening caller was full of spite, he had little in the way of intelligence.

I immediately contacted the Federal Protective Service. Within hours, law enforcement appeared at the suspect's residence to question him. His name is inconsequential, but you should know this: he was an intolerant forty-seven-year-old White homosexual male with a long history of diagnosed mental disorders, assaultive behavior, and making threats.

THE ARREST

During his questioning by numerous law-enforcement agencies, the man admitted to making the telephone calls and the threats but denied that he would ever hurt anyone. I was told by law enforcement that he had an anxiety disorder and was clinically diagnosed as mentally ill, but refused medication. They also told me that he believed he was superior to others, and he hated "Asians, women, Blacks and Italians." The one woman agent who interviewed him stated that she could feel the hate rise within him when speaking about these targeted groups of people.

What happened next was the first in a series of legal episodes that absolutely dumbfounded me. I was informed by the investigating law-enforcement agent that the U.S. attorney's office was not going to charge the suspect due to a lack of paperwork. I was stunned; this man had confessed. Law enforcement was going to attempt to detain the suspect on a seventy-two-hour psychiatric-evaluation hold. They told me that under the circumstances it was the best they could do.

I got on the telephone and began calling the Department of Justice. A good friend of mine who was an attorney practicing in criminal law called the local U.S. attorney's office.

The federal agent investigating the crime called again and told me he felt that this man posed a real danger to our safety and, for this reason, he was going to put a longer federal hold on the suspect, and would deal with the consequences later.

Relief.

Immediately thereafter, I learned that the U.S. attorney's office was, after all, going to file charges against the suspect.

BAIL

Eleven days after the suspect's arrest, I received another phone call. This one came from one of the investigating federal agents. The suspect had had a bail and detention hearing in federal court, and the court was releasing him on a surety bond of fifty thousand dollars, posted by his employer, with the requirement that he remain in a halfway house until his preliminary court hearing two weeks later. It was the court's feeling that, despite the suspect's twenty-five-year criminal history, the charges were only misdemeanors and thus warranted bail and restricted release. I was speechless and my stomach turned.

After spending the entire day worrying, I received a second telephone call from the same agent, who informed me that the suspect would be remaining in custody until a hearing the next morning. Neither of the two halfway houses in the Bay Area would accept him. I told the agent that I would be present the next morning.

THE CHARGES

For the next eight months, I attended every court hearing on the case.

The hate-crimes perpetrator, now the defendant, was being charged solely with threatening a public official. The complaint contained no mention of the third telephone call—the one he'd left on my voice mail—or of any hate-crime charge.

I later learned that none of the hate language and none of the suspect's references to ethnicity or gender were included in the complaint because the agent felt that such references would be "offensive" and were unnecessary to the prosecuted charge.

From the little I had read about hate crimes and the law, I thought that certainly a hate crime should be charged in this case.

The elements all seemed to be present: an act of intimidation, harassment, and a threat of physical injury motivated by the suspect's hostility to the victim's race, ethnic background, and gender, with the intention of causing fear or intimidation and wholly to deter the free exercise of enjoyment of rights and privileges secured by the Constitution and the laws of the United States.

Little did I know then that I was wrong. I had so much to learn.

I am very fortunate that I have great friends, who are also brilliant attorneys, to advise me. At the second bail hearing, on August 10, my support group strategized two goals: one, to keep the defendant incarcerated; and two, to pursue a hate-crime charge. As we sat outside the courtroom, we discussed a number of different options, including putting together a community forum to speak with the U.S. attorney's office. We also discussed suggesting to the court that the defendant be put on electronic monitoring rather than restricted release.

When the prosecuting assistant U.S. attorney (AUSA) arrived, I introduced myself and my colleagues. We sat down on a wooden bench outside the courtroom and began to talk about the case. I told him that I was concerned because there was no hate-crime charge in the complaint. I asked him if he had heard the third taped voice-mail message. He said he had read about it, and he listened to me as I told him the contents of the message and how scared I was at the possibility that the defendant would be released with restrictions. I sat there on that bench and I cried.

When we walked into the courtroom I was surprised to see that the defendant was being represented by a federal public defender who was African American. In the ongoing weeks the defendant would request and receive a pro bono criminal-defense panel attorney to represent him because he did not feel he could trust the governmental bureaucracy of the public-defender's office. I think the federal public defender represented the defendant very well, that it was the defendant's loss to change attorneys, and that the real reason behind the change was bigotry.

I was also surprised at the defendant's appearance. Although he was aggressive and hateful, threatening on the phone to slash throats, in person he was a small, thin man, about five feet, six inches tall, with brown eyes and hair and wearing wire-rimmed glasses.

When our case came before the court, the prosecutor made his case well. He told the court that he had spoken to numerous people at my office who had stated that they felt this man was a real threat and had expressed their fear of him. He also got the court to agree to let him play in open court the tape recording of the voice-mail message left on my machine.

Two representatives from the Bay Area halfway houses told the court that they refused to take the defendant in because he had a history of assault and battery and that they questioned his mental stability without a psychological evaluation. The judge stated that he had concerns for the safety of the community and ordered the defendant to remain in custody pending a psychological evaluation. Finally, a break.

I learned a few frightening things about the defendant during the bail hearing. The prosecutor stated that the defendant had a twenty-five-year history of threatening people, assaulting people, and committing batteries. He had been convicted of third-degree assault in 1993 and was committed to a psychiatric institution. He had threatened the lives of Nancy Reagan, Barbara Bush, and the Bush children. In 1994 he assaulted a worker at San Francisco Community College, and in 1995 he spat at and threw a piece of wood at a Walgreen's clerk, hitting the victim in the mouth. He had continually committed the same acts, always with the promise never to do them again.

HATE CRIMES: THE FEDERAL LAW

In the week following the hearing, I began to better educate myself about the different federal and state hate-crime laws and what requirements must be met to charge a hate crime. I discovered that although the state of California had a very progressive and encompassing hate-crime law, the federal hate-crime law was extremely narrow in scope. (Since federal law preempts state law, no charges would be brought in a state court in this case.)

For a hate crime to be charged under the federal statute, Title 18 of the United States Code at Section 245(b), the federal government must prove both that the crime occurred because of a victim's race, color, religion, or national origin and that it happened *because* (not simply *while*) the victim was engaged in one of six narrowly defined federally protected activities, such as serving on a jury or attending a public school. In addition, before a federal hate crime can be charged, authorization must be obtained from the U.S. Department of Justice.

I began meeting and communicating with the AUSA's office, the U.S. Department of Justice, and community leaders from the South Asian Bar Association, the Mexican American Legal Defense and Education Fund, the Coalition United Against Violence (CUAV), the Lawyers' Committee for Civil Rights of the San Francisco Bay Area, and the Asian Law Caucus—all in an effort to determine if a hate crime could be charged against the defendant. The AUSA's office was very open, candid, and educational in meeting with the community regarding this case. We all knew the limitations of the federal hate-crime law and worked together to try to find a way to charge a hate crime in this case.

The office of the U.S. Commission on Civil Rights also became proactive in the movement to pass the 1999 Hate Crimes Prevention Act, which would have broadened the current law by eliminating the victim's required participation in a federally protected activity and expanded protections to victims of hate crimes based upon their sexual orientation, gender, or disability. This effort was thwarted in Congress in 1999.

By August 20, 1999, no hate crime had been charged, and the case was scheduled to proceed to the grand jury within the week. The prosecutor said he did not understand all of the "fuss" that was being made. We tried to convey how hate crimes not only affect the individual victim but also have a chilling effect upon the entire targeted community. The bottom line, however, was that a federal hate crime was not going to be charged in my case. The facts were just not there, and the statute was too narrow; even though the defendant had made threats based upon gender and ethnicity, gender was not a protected category, and we were not engaged in one of the six federally protected activities.

In addition, from the standpoint of strategy, the AUSA correctly worried about the effect on a jury of bringing a hate-crime charge. The facts of my case warranted only a misdemeanor hate-crime charge. The AUSA made an analogy to the wise King Solomon: if a felony charge of threatening a public official and a misdemeanor hate-crime charge were put before a jury, the fear was that the jury would "split the baby" and convict on the hate-crime misdemeanor, which would carry no jail time.

On November 1, I had a telephone conversation with one of my attorneys and let him know that I absolutely did not want to testify in open court before the defendant at a trial. The thought of putting myself in front of him and becoming his next target did not appeal to me at all. Every time I thought about it, I had serious fears of his sitting in his jail cell remembering it was me who pointed the finger that identified him. My attorney advised that I not reveal this to the AUSA because it could affect his plea-bargaining stance if he thought he might have an uncooperative witness on his hands. I agreed.

On November 23, at the trial-setting conference, the AUSA informed the court that his office would be seeking a hate-crime sentencing enhancement pursuant to the Federal Sentencing Guidelines. The maximum statutory penalty was three years in federal prison and a fine of $250,000. Again, this was the best that could be done given the limitations the AUSA's office faced under the current, limited federal hate-crime legislation.

The defendant spoke at this hearing. I listened as he requested to be transferred to another prison facility, because he'd had to be put into solitary "for his own protection." Apparently, while in the general population, he'd made an intolerant comment to two other inmates and now was fearful himself. Some justice.

The next week, I attended the pretrial hearing and was served with a subpoena to testify at trial, set for December 6. The prosecution and the defense informed the court that they were close to working out a plea agreement to forego trial, and requested that the hearing be continued until the next day. The court agreed. I reiterated to my attorney that I absolutely did not want to testify. Although my fear had been only intermittent throughout the preceding four months, it began to rise again, and I was a wreck for the next twenty-four hours.

To my relief, on December 1, 1999, the prosecution and the defendant entered into a plea agreement including the hate-crime sentencing enhancement. I would not have to testify at trial. I should note that my friend and attorney advisor attended every single hearing with me. No matter how short the notice, whether two weeks or one day, he carved out time from his schedule to support and advise me, and for this I was truly appreciative—especially on December 1. I told my friend that I could handle it without him if his schedule was too busy, but as I sat there alone in the huge federal courtroom, I began to shake out of fear. I was so grateful and relieved when he arrived.

We listened to the court thoroughly engage the defendant to ensure that he understood the nature and effect of the plea agreement and what he was pleading guilty to. The courtroom was silent except for their exchange; hearing this man again retell explicitly the threats he'd made and why was excruciating to me.

I later read the plea agreement, which stated that the defendant admitted to threatening a public official, and that he'd selected his victims because of their gender and ethnicity. The agreement further stated that the prosecution would seek a base offense level of 12, adjusted to level 13 with the hate-crime enhancement, and would seek the low end of the guidelines. I had no idea what this meant until a few months later. Sentencing was scheduled for February, and the defendant was to remain incarcerated until then, so I breathed a bit easier for a time.

SENTENCING

As sentencing day approached, the AUSA's office informed me that I as a victim had a right to address the court regarding the sentencing, either in person or in writing. The office also sent over a victim-impact-statement form for cases of violent crime. I came to understand the importance of the plea agreement with regard to sentencing: level 13 meant that the prosecution would be requesting that the defendant be incarcerated for twelve to eighteen months, not the maximum three years.

The federal probation officer also telephoned me and requested that I tell her how the case had impacted my life. She told me that she felt the defendant was an actual danger to my office and that the defendant had a history of assaulting women and men who were smaller than he. In later conversations, she told me that based upon her interview with the defendant, her review of his twenty-five-year history of assault, battery, and mental considerations, and her conversations with all of the victims, she was going to recommend that the court not comply with the plea agreement but instead sentence the defendant to the full three-year maximum. That seemed fine to me. The more time, the better. She asked if I would like to address the court. I told her I would have to consult my attorneys.

One of the calls I made was to the AUSA. I asked the attorney if he thought it would assist the sentencing process if I addressed the court at sentencing. I learned then that a difference of opinion existed between the AUSA's plea agreement and the probation officer's recommendation. If the court decided in its discretion to agree with the probation officer and sentence the defendant to three years, this would constitute a substantial departure from the plea agreement, and the defendant would be within his rights to revoke the plea agreement and go to trial. Again I felt stunned and conflicted—of course I wanted this threatening man incarcerated for as long a period as possible, but at the expense of putting myself out there and testifying?

Then, through the federal probation office, I received an "apology letter" written by the defendant. It was addressed not to any of his victims but to his attorney. He apologized for anyone he'd hurt, "at least in part." He went on to state that his actions were "foolishness" and that he didn't realize his actions would victimize anyone. He regretted "not thinking before speaking," excused himself for any "presumptions," and stated that he was sincerely "ready to atone further" for his wrongs. If this was intended as an apology letter to his victims, it was the most insincere apology I have ever encountered. In fact, it was not an apology letter at all; it was an exercise for the benefit of sentencing. That he didn't realize his actions would victimize is ludicrous— he had a twenty-five-year criminal history of repeatedly making threats, and of committing assault and battery. I am sure, however, that he must have regretted not thinking before speaking— he was in an orange jumpsuit sitting in federal prison.

I decided once more I did not feel comfortable addressing the court in front of the defendant, no matter how much he had affected my life. I planned to attend the sentencing and then get on with my life.

At the sentencing hearing, both the AUSA and the federal probation officer made their recommendations, and the judge went through the defendant's objections to the presentencing report. The judge stated that this case was a level 14 with a criminal history of level 2, which would put the defendant's sentence at eighteen to twenty-four months in federal prison. He also stated that, although he appreciated the upward recommendation of three years for sentencing made by the federal probation officer, it was the government who had the responsibility of reviewing the case and making the recommendation. The court sentenced the defendant to eighteen months in federal prison with a one-year supervised release. Thanks to the federal probation officer, the judge also required the defendant to do one hundred hours of community service and enroll in a mental health/treatment program.

The defendant did not speak at all. At the end of the hearing, however, his attorney requested that the court recommend that he be confined in a federal prison in the state of Oregon because he had a male "friend" in that area. When the judge questioned the defense attorney about the nature of the relationship between the defendant and his male friend to support his making such a recommendation, the attorney stated that the defendant felt "uncomfortable talking about it in open court." It seems strange that on the one hand this defendant is a gay male who recognizes what it is to be a minority and declines to discuss his sexual orientation, and on the other hand he has the audacity and the aggressiveness to violently threaten other minorities who cannot hide their race or their gender.

CLOSURE

Through this experience, I have learned so much about the law, the strength of many communities, the support of good friends, and the lesson of moving on. My case is over and my life has resumed, and I continue to advocate against hate crimes, support stronger hate-crime legislation, and help to educate the community.

2

The Interrelationship between Anti-Asian Violence and Asian America

Victor M. Hwang

INTRODUCTION

The concept of the Asian Pacific American community is unique in the field of American race relations. Our community is united neither by a common experience such as slavery nor by a common language such as Spanish. We are individually Vietnamese Amerasians, second-generation South Asian Americans, refugees, Sansei children of internees (Japanese Americans, third generation), Korean Americans, FOBs (fresh off the boat), JOJs (just off the jet), Filipino seniors, hapas (APIs of mixed racial heritage), Taiwanese nationalists, and more. In many ways, the Hmong veteran escaping persecution from Laos may have much more in common with the political refugee from Guatemala in terms of language and cultural barriers, moral and family values, psychological trauma, job skills, and education than with a third-generation Japanese American who grew up in Gardena. The Taiwanese software salesman may identify closer along class and political interests with the German transnational machine-parts manufacturer than with a second-generation Cantonese seamstress in Chinatown. Our community encompasses differences in ethnicity, religion, language, culture, class, color, immigration history, politics, and even race.

43

What we do have most obviously in common is the way we look to those outside our community and the way we are treated in North America based upon the way we look. Our commonality begins with a recognition that whether you are a first-generation Vietnamese American rollerblading at a park or a second-generation Chinese American celebrating your bachelor party, you are constantly at risk of being killed without warning or provocation based upon the belief that you are a foreign "Jap." Whether you are a second-generation South Asian American or a fifth-generation Chinatown native, you are faced constantly with the implicit and explicit question, "No, really, where are you from?"

Yet, while anti-Asian violence forces individuals to band together at times for physical or political protection, it plays a much greater role in shaping the Asian Pacific American community than simply being the outside threat that drives the flock together. It is not the action of anti-Asian violence that is so important to the development of our community as much as it is the reaction to the incident. For Asian Pacific America lives not in the Chinatowns or the Little Tokyos but in the hearts of those who recognize that incidents of anti-Asian violence are not random or isolated attacks, but rather a part and practice of the historical treatment of Asian Pacifics in America for the past two hundred years.

As much as immigration and antimiscegenation laws have worked hand in hand to control and manipulate the number of Asian immigrants in the United States to serve the needs of labor, the pattern of anti-Asian violence has dictated the role and character of our community and its relationship to mainstream society. From the unofficially sanctioned massacres of Chinese in mining camps to laws prohibiting the testimony of Chinese witnesses in courts against the murderers, the unspoken policy and history of the United States has been to erase the experience of Asians in America and to silence the voice of the community. Thus we have been displaced from our role in U.S. history, from our place in America, and more than two hundred years after the first Asians came to America, we are still being collectively told to go back to where we came from.

It is in our struggle against this pattern of violence and its underlying message of physical, political, and historical exclusion that we find ourselves as Asian Pacific Americans. Not every

Asian in the United States is a member of the Asian Pacific American community. We are born or naturalized as Americans by geographic and legal definitions, and we can be distinguished as Asians based upon certain physiological and racial characteristics. But we become Asian Americans as we begin to recognize that we share a common bond and experience with all other Asians in America based upon our history, our treatment, and our status as a racial minority in the United States. The formation of the community begins not when ten Asian families happen to live in the same neighborhood, but when one family has been attacked and the other nine rally to its assistance.

The Asian American community is based on an understanding of and appreciation for the fact that we have struggled for nearly two centuries against this violence and exclusion in the plantations, in the courts, and on the battlefields. From the early organizing efforts of the Chinese Six Companies in San Francisco to protect the Chinese workers from nativist attacks to the more recent campaigns to bring justice to the killers of Vincent Chin and Kao Kuan Chung, Asian Americans have not always been the silent victims of hate crimes but have strived to defend and empower our communities in the American tradition.

This chapter will discuss the role of anti-Asian violence as a foil and as a catalyst in the development of an Asian American identity and community. Our community lives in the contradiction, in the friction between competing notions of ethnicity and nationality, in the margins and as a wedge between Black and White in American society. It is not a physical community, but one that exists in flashes, in movements, in speeches, in hearts and minds, and in struggle. It is within the heat of the response to these incidents of extreme racial violence that we continue to forge our identity and our sense of community. We build our community in times of crisis by speaking out against incidents of anti-Asian violence and claiming our piece of history.

However, in times of racial tension, it is sometimes difficult to parse and process the elements of the hate crime to craft an effective and targeted response that both serves the needs of the individual victim and empowers the community. In this paper, I will explore two recent incidents of anti-Asian violence as a framework for discussing the crafting and miscrafting of a progressive community response. For in responding to a hate crime, like any good doctor, we need to understand the nature of the injury and who has been hurt before we begin diagnosing a solution. Without an understanding of the history of anti-Asian violence, hate crimes, and the community, we can do little for either the protection of the individual or the development of Asian America.

ANTI-ASIAN VIOLENCE AND THE INDIVIDUAL: WHAT IS THE INJURY?

Individual victims of hate crimes and their families often suffer injuries far beyond the physical wounds inflicted upon them. Unlike the children's mantra, it is both the sticks and stones that break our bones and the accompanying words and hateful intent that hurt us. Like a snake's bite, the venomous injuries of anti-Asian violence go far deeper than the superficial injury because they are intended to inject a poison to strike at the core of our being. As advocates, we must recognize the injury to the internal psyche as well as the physical injury in crafting a remedy for the individual and the community. As much as you cannot treat a snake bite with a Band-Aid, you cannot treat the hate crime as either a simple crime or an accident.

The Incident

Sylvia Kim is a Korean American sixty-three years young who came to the United States as a teenager. She grew up in Washington, D.C., the daughter of a Korean minister, and attended an all-White segregated high school.

She spent most of her adult years in Arizona as the wife of a university professor, where, she never thought she experienced much racism in the ivory-tower setting. "Oh, every once in a while, my kids would tell me that someone had called them a Chinaman in school or had tried to put them down on account of their race," she said. "But I always told them just to work harder and prove to every one else that they were superior. I knew that we were descendants of a proud people with many centuries of culture and civilization. I never worried much about what the other people thought. I knew we were better."

She never had much contact with African Americans, but says that she always sort of looked down her nose at them since she felt they tended to complain too much about racism and failed to adopt the Asian work ethic to work twice as hard when confronted with racist behavior.

Sylvia moved to California a number of years ago, and ironically it was in San Francisco that she experienced her first taste of anti-Asian violence. She was coming out of the Borders bookstore in Union Square when a six-foot-tall "Timothy McVeigh"–looking Caucasian man ran up to her and said, "My mother is not Chinese but yours is." Sylvia was somewhat taken aback and said, "What?" She tried to ignore him and pass him by.

He repeated the remark from behind her, and when she did not react he picked her up from behind and threw her against a nearby concrete wall, shattering her hip. Her assailant then ran away. As she lay there in shock she was assaulted again in a much more painful and personal way as two Caucasian tourists walked by and—trying to be helpful—asked her if she spoke English.

"I was so outraged then, I couldn't even respond. Here I lay, on the ground; I was beaten, my hip was shattered, and the first thing they asked me was if I spoke English, not if I was okay, if I needed help, or if they should call an ambulance. The first thing they asked me was if I spoke English—and they were clearly tourists. I was so shocked, I couldn't say anything."

Even in an emergency situation, Sylvia noted afterwards, the first thought that passed through the minds of those Caucasians upon seeing an injured Asian woman was not the injury, but the race.

Sylvia was eventually taken to the hospital and underwent extensive surgery to have her entire hip replaced. But as her physical injuries were treated by the doctors and healed, her psychological injuries remained unattended, and they festered until she fell into a deep depression.

"My coworkers, who were mostly Caucasian, came by to see me, and I guess they were trying to be funny. One of them said something like, 'Well, at least you got a new hip.' At that moment, I just felt so angry that they couldn't understand that I was almost killed because of my race. I just didn't think I could ever see them in the same light again.

"They had a hard time saying *assault*; they felt embarrassed and responsible," according to Sylvia. "The first thing they asked was, 'Did he take your money?'" Her friends felt that she was obsessed with the racial nature of the attack and that she should not dwell on the incident. Sylvia, on the other hand, felt like she wasn't able to talk with them anymore.

The police talked to a few witnesses but were unable to develop any substantive leads. In the opinion of Sylvia's family, the police discouraged them from pursuing an active criminal investigation. Time and again Sylvia was told by the police officer in charge of the investigation that it was not worth pursuing the assailant; better to forget the incident and simply let old wounds heal. Though witnesses indicated that the assailant had been hanging around the area previously and had harassed other people of color, the police closed their investigation shortly after the incident.

As time progressed, Sylvia did not just "get over" the racial attack; instead, her mental health continued to deteriorate to the point where the family contacted the Asian Law Caucus and expressed grave concerns over her well-being. They were frustrated over the lack of police response, angry over the racist nature of the attack, and distressed over Sylvia's deepening depression.

I spoke initially with Sylvia a few weeks after the incident and made some inquiries with the police regarding the status of her case. Although this clearly constituted a hate crime and had been treated as such by the police department, as is the case with the overwhelming majority of hate crimes, there was little the criminal-justice system could do since the assailant had not been caught. The police expressed a general resistance to conducting any additional investigation into Sylvia's case, stating their opinion that taking further action would prove hopeless since it had been a random assault.

Sylvia felt that getting her story into the media would encourage greater interest in her case and help her talk through what had happened to her. I helped her do this.

The Response: What Is the Injury?

By treating only her physical injuries, the doctors treated Sylvia the same way they would have handled a patient who had fallen down the stairs or who had been in an automobile accident.

While they were able to replace her shattered hip, they did not even attempt to replace the shattered frame of reference that had helped her throughout life to interpret, deflect, and respond to racism. Without warning, she had been inexplicably attacked—and her life drastically changed—all by an idea that she had tried to suppress or ignore for most of her life. In failing to address the underlying cause of the injury, her doctors failed to treat the most serious injury of all: the one to her psyche. Sylvia was left feeling confused and powerless, without the ability to either explain or prevent another unprovoked attack.

The isolated hate crime is particularly venomous because of its seemingly random nature and the inability of the victim to rationalize its occurrence. Even as children, we learn to create mental defenses and white lies to guard against mental attacks from others. Rationalization is an important defense in our logical world, and as thinking beings, it is important for us to believe that the world is controlled by rationality. By assigning reasons to why bad things happen, we can learn from our experiences and change to avoid a reoccurrence. The inability to explain the incident therefore subjects the victim to further trauma, because if you can't explain it, there's nothing you can do to prevent it from happening to you again. The well-documented tendency of victims to blame themselves can often be mitigated by a belief that a change in behavior will prevent the occurrence from happening again. We like to think of life events as cause and effect, order out of chaos.

A victim of a burglary may rationalize that he had not taken enough safety precautions and then install a better alarm system. Someone who is involved in an automobile accident will try to remember to look both ways next time before crossing the street. But there is nothing you can do to hide your race, skin color, gender, or to some extent sexual orientation. There is simply no escape or change in behavior possible for these victims, so they understand that they have to live with the possibility of recurrence without warning. In Sylvia's case and many similar cases, this helplessness may be exacerbated by the fact that the perpetrators are rarely caught.

Moreover, feelings of helplessness may be compounded by the fact that the victim may never even have viewed himself or herself as a representative of a community. As victims of hate crimes, they are subject to attack not as an individual but as a symbol. They are stripped of their individuality, their person-hood, and they are reduced to their race. As Sylvia was being at-tacked, her assailant kept repeating, "My mother is not Chinese, but yours is." Sylvia was not attacked for anything about her, anything she stood for, but on the basis of her birth into a (per-ceived) Chinese family. Her "crime" in the eyes of the attacker was not of *acting* Chinese or even *being* Chinese, but was the crime of her ancestors in being born Chinese. The message was direct and terrifying: you are different from me and so I must hurt you.

This is the poison of hate crimes that distinguishes them from other types of victimization. Often, the person is being attacked not as an individual, but merely to set an example for the rest of the community. The consistent message of violence directed against Asian Pacific Americans is: you are the foreigner, you do not belong here, you are not an American.

This message was one that Sylvia was ill prepared to receive. It violently contradicted all of the promises of America that she had been raised to believe and that she had adopted as her own values. Like many immigrants, Sylvia had always firmly be-lieved in the ideal of America as the land of equality and oppor-tunity. If you worked hard, you could get ahead, blend in, and be considered an equal. In the instances where she or her family was confronted with racist attitudes, her external response was to work twice as hard to go around the wall of racism, to work harder to prove her worth as an American.

Such is the response of many immigrants who choose to ac-cept the burden of racism when confronted with it instead of standing on their rights as newer but equal Americans. In com-ing to America, they accept the unspoken racial hierarchy that will allow Asians to succeed to the point where they hit the glass ceiling. They do not even carry the expectations of parity with Whites. As such, they are identified as the "model minority," willing to accept a second-class standard of living, as contrasted with African Americans, whose civil-rights paradigm has de-manded an equal playing field or they will not play at all. As with Sylvia, this is precisely why many immigrants look down upon African Americans: because they themselves have made the difficult choice to swallow their pride and accept their status in order to provide their children with a better future. Sylvia believed that African Americans chose to complain too much and didn't work hard enough to fight their way through the wall of racism.

However, the attack shook Sylvia to the core not only due to its extreme violence but also because it forced her to confront the fact that regardless of the years of work she put into proving herself and her children, goodwill offered her little protection from either the attacker or the tourists—both of whom would never view her as an equal American. In an incident lasting less than a minute, one man stripped her of her veneer, her status as an honorary White, and reduced her to her race. Despite years of sacrifice and hard work to form a protective layer of class, assimilation, and privilege, she understood now that she was still as vulnerable as the newly arrived Asian immigrant or the African American. And as Sylvia discovered, you could not just turn your back and try to ignore the racism; it would follow you and haunt you. The advice that she had given herself and her children for years simply didn't work; it failed to protect her from brutal assault.

The attack also undermined Sylvia's second learned form of psychological defense: the internal strength she gained against racist attacks by relying upon her heritage as a Korean immigrant. Sylvia had been able to disregard less severe incidents and dismiss the rejection by falling back upon her identification with Korean culture. As a first-generation immigrant with some grounding in the Korean culture, she was able to draw strength from the idea that in her true home, she would be regarded as an equal, that in America, as a guest or sojourner, she could accept second-class citizenship. This is a standard form of mental gamesmanship that we all engage in to protect our sense of pride. When denied a certain goal we will create the lie that we didn't really want it anyway. I don't deserve to be treated like a regular American and I don't need to respond to these demeaning attitudes because I have another home in Korea where they treat me like an equal.

However, perhaps due to the passage of time and the length of her tenure in the United States, or perhaps due to the seriousness of her injuries, Sylvia was no longer able to ignore the fact that her rights had been violated and that she was not respected as an equal in the country where she had spent the majority of her life. Although Sylvia was originally an immigrant, her fifty years of struggle and survival here in the United States had earned her the right to be recognized as an American, equal and unquestioned. But now, only moments after her physical assault, she was assaulted again verbally by well-meaning passersby who questioned her identity even before asking about her injuries. By skinhead and good Samaritan, she was viewed as a foreigner, as an outsider, told physically and orally that she did not belong.

Sylvia's inability to use her birthplace heritage as a source of comfort was a first step toward establishing an identity as an Asian American. The birth of the Asian Pacific American identity begins when the standard tag of "Oh, you speak English so well (for a foreigner)" is no longer considered a compliment but taken as an insult. However, at this point, lacking a further bridge to developing an Asian American consciousness, she knew only that a door had closed behind her without yet seeing a path before her. Lost and feeling abandoned, Sylvia fell into a depression over the realization that she was homeless, neither Korean nor American. In this netherworld, she could no longer claim either the protection of her cultural heritage or the promise of American equality.

Sylvia's Response: Knocking Down Walls and Hipper than Ever

Metaphorically speaking, Sylvia had been thrown against the concrete wall of racial reality. This had forced her to reexamine her internal and external defenses, which she had previously erected to deny or mitigate the existence of racism in her life. In a context far beyond the racial taunts suffered by her children, the seriousness of the injury forced her into a position where she could no longer dismiss the prejudice as irrelevant. The life-threatening nature of her injuries forced her to take a second look not only at racism, but at her own past responses and attitudes.

Sylvia's response as she gradually healed was to build an entirely new frame of reference for relating to American society, one that incorporated elements of Asian American and cross-cultural studies.

Ironically, at the time that she was subjected to this hate violence, Sylvia had been taking a class in cross-cultural studies to become a certified ESL instructor. She had actually gone to the bookstore that day to buy some of the books assigned for the class. She tells me that initially she hadn't put much stock in the class and found many of the African American attitudes to be tiresome. *"Why couldn't they just work harder? I thought. Why do they always complain so much?"*

But as she lay in her hospital bed, one of the African American students from her class made a special point to visit her. She watched as he was stopped by the hospital staff and questioned about his reasons for being at the hospital, and she noted how he politely and insistently dealt with the situation. As he made his way to her bed and held her hand, Sylvia began to cry, and she cried like she could never stop.

"All I could say to him was, 'I'm sorry, I'm sorry, only now can I begin to understand.'"

Although her attacker had been Caucasian, the attack prompted her to reexamine her beliefs and attitudes toward all race relations, with a particular emphasis on African Americans. By turning to the theories she had encountered in cross-racial-studies courses, she found a framework for recovery, a new structure for reevaluating her own life and experiences through the lens of race. In her attack, that which had been theoretical and incomprehensible found form and substance, and what had previously existed outside her reality she now embraced as her point of view. She read books on Martin Luther King Jr. and other African American leaders, looking to them for answers as the "model minority."

As she began to understand the broader context of racism and race relations in the United States, her incident of hate violence began to seem less and less a random occurrence. At the same time, it became less painful as she read about the history of African Americans in the United States. "I just stopped feeling sorry for myself. After all, it had only happened to me a few times. But this sort of thing was happening to African Americans all the time. I just told myself to get over it."

Talking with her children and other people about her experiences and her newfound framework, she eagerly embraced learning about new cultures and new ideas. It was as if she were born again at the age of sixty-three. She tells me how, recently, while watching the documentary *Once We Were Kings*, regarding the life of boxing champion Muhammad Ali, she again broke down weeping in the theater.

"I grew up hearing about this Muhammad Ali, and to tell you the truth, we always sort of looked down on him. In the Korean culture, we don't respect physical accomplishments that much—perhaps it is the Confucian teachings, which tell us to respect that which you can accomplish with your brain.

"But now, for the first time, I understand the courage and honor of Muhammad Ali in changing his name and taking a stand for his people. I used to think of him as a braggart. Now I see him as a hero. I never knew he risked so much. In a way, my biggest regret is that this beating I suffered didn't happen to me sixty years earlier," she laughs. "I now look back on my life and think how blind I was. I now spend time reflecting on my whole life and I think what I might have done different if only my eyes had been opened sooner to the racism in our society. I wish I had been able to do more about it."

Sylvia credits her exploration and increased understanding of the African American struggle with providing her the strength and context to fight her way out of the pit of depression. "I don't hate White people; I still don't know that much about Black people, but I know more now about where I fit in than I did before."

Sylvia has recovered both physically and psychologically and continues to attend classes exploring race relations and cultural studies. After the release of the 1996 National Asian Pacific American Legal Consortium report on violence against Asian Pacific Americans, Sylvia was profiled widely by the media, including an appearance on the *MacNeil/Lehrer NewsHour*. She hopes to be certified as an ESL instructor soon. She intends to teach new immigrants not only about English, but about America.

SWASTIKAS IN THE SUNSET: WHO IS THE VICTIM?

The Incident

The Sunset District of San Francisco is an affordable residential and small-business community located in the western section of the city, running along Golden Gate Park along Irving and Judah Streets. It is a culturally diverse and middle-class neighborhood with a long-established Jewish Russian community and a rapidly growing Asian American immigrant population. The Asian American population of the Sunset District has doubled in recent years, and many now refer to the area as the New Chinatown. The area has historically prided itself on its neighborhood "mom and pop" stores and has been highly resistant to the influx of chain stores and fast-food franchises.

In 1996, a Chinese American business owner opened a Burger King franchise in the area, which was immediately met with community resistance, both reasoned and racist. While some residents protested the change in the neighborhood character, others posted flyers calling for "Chinks and Burger King Out of the Sunset." The Burger King was subject to a barrage of vandalism, graffiti, and protests throughout the following months, continuing to the present day.

In February of 1997, an individual or a group of individuals known as the SWB or "Sunset White Boys" carved swastikas into the glass storefronts of nearly two dozen Asian American businesses, mostly along Irving Street. The placement and selectivity of the swastikas were particularly ominous, in that primarily Asian-owned businesses were targeted and non-Asian businesses were passed over, with the exception of a Caucasian-run karate studio with Asian lettering on the storefront. The clinical precision exercised in the choice of the targets not only indicated a familiarity with the community, leading people to suspect that this was an "inside" job, but carried the biblical overtones of genocide and divine retribution.

The vandalism ranged from small red spray-painted swastikas accompanied by the initials SWB to three-foot-high swastikas carved with great force into the glass using some sharp instrument. A great deal of attention and energy were focused in particular upon the Bank of the Orient, with the swastika carved prominently next to the word Orient.

Surprisingly, many of the store owners were immigrants from China and Vietnam who confessed ignorance at the significance of the swastikas. All they knew was that they had been vandalized once again, and due to the indifferent or hostile treatment that they had received at the hands of the police in previous cases of vandalism, most failed to even report the occurrence. Many did not realize that other Asian businesses along the street had suffered similar etchings, and more than a week passed without any action being taken; the swastikas remained prominently displayed to the public.

The swastikas were finally brought to the attention of a Chinese American police officer in another jurisdiction who decided to look into it on his own. The Asian Law Caucus was notified through a third-hand source during the course of the investigation and immediately visited the location to document the hate vandalism, and to interview and offer assistance to the targeted merchants. On two different occasions, staff and volunteers walked up and down Irving Street, meeting with each of the merchants as well as with customers and people in the street.

Even after I spoke with them, some of the store owners indicated that they did not intend to replace the glass panes defaced with swastikas since vandalism was rampant and they would just be hit again after spending the money. It was chilling to see customers and families coming to the area to shop or do business as usual in broad daylight with each of the storefronts marked by the violent emblems.

Many of the merchants were reluctant to have their businesses photographed or identified for fear of retaliation, and many expressed surprise that what they viewed as another routine round of vandalism had attracted outside attention. After we completed speaking with the victim-merchants and documented the incidents, we alerted the mainstream press. Both print and broadcast media ran widespread coverage on the swastikas even though the vandalism had taken place up to a week earlier. In reaction to the press coverage and the public outcry, the police and elected officials hastened to respond.

The Response: Who Is the Victim?

The response to a hate crime must be carefully tailored to address the needs and concerns both of the primary victim and of the community. A directed and strategic response works to counter the hateful message of exclusion and intimidation. However, in many cases, such as this one, it remains unclear at the outset who the primary victim is and toward whom the communal remedy should be directed. Was the true victim of the hate crime the more established Jewish community at large, which was forced to confront the painful reminder of the Holocaust? Or was the victim the potential APA store owner, resident, or customer considering coming into the Sunset District but then scared away by the prospect of being targeted because of his or her ethnicity? Or was it the San Francisco community at large? The responses of various authorities in this case differed depending upon their determination of who the victim was. While all were successful in achieving some measure of combating hate crimes, no one fully addressed the underlying tensions that created the hate-filled environment.

The Police Response

Typically, the police focus solely on the apprehension of the criminal and exhibit little sympathy toward or understanding of the needs of the victim or the community. Generally, they are reluctant to categorize any case as a hate crime, perhaps out of an unwillingness to invest the extra time to conduct additional investigation, or perhaps due to a resistance to taint their jurisdiction with the insinuation of racism.

In this case, the police responded exceptionally poorly, which was surprising given the fact that San Francisco Police Department Chief Fred Lau is Chinese American and the department has maintained for years a separate investigative unit specially trained and devoted to working on hate crimes. In response to press inquiries, the police captain of the district incredulously countered that these carvings were not hate crimes since swastikas are anti-Jew in nature and not anti-Asian. While this initial statement was quickly retracted, the captain's later position would be that these acts of vandalism were the acts of juveniles and therefore not to be taken seriously. The acts were dismissed and somehow excused as childish pranks and therefore not worthy of community discussion and intervention.

Under increasing scrutiny and public pressure, Chief Fred Lau intervened, and several bilingual officers were reassigned to patrol the Sunset District. The case was turned over to the special hate-crimes unit, and general police presence in the area was increased over the short term in an attempt to apprehend the perpetrator(s).

Several juveniles were soon arrested, and newspaper headlines reported that the responsible parties had been found, case closed. Conveniently, one of the youths was Filipino, and so the police took the opportunity to declare that this clearly did not constitute a hate crime since one of the suspects was Asian. Weeks later, with much less fanfare, it was reported that the youths who were arrested—while admitting to general tagging in the neighborhood—did not actually have anything to do with the swastikas.

When community and media pressure died down after a few weeks, nothing further was heard from the police regarding their efforts to find the perpetrators.

Asian American Merchants As Victims?

One Asian American San Francisco county supervisor organized a highly successful volunteer cleanup day and recruited elected officials, union labor, donations of materials, and community members to clean up all of the graffiti, sweep the streets, and replace the glass at no charge to the victim-merchants. Volunteers turned out from all parts of the city with great media fanfare that succeeded in literally whitewashing the hate from public view. The event removed the obvious signs of hate and arguably sent a message to the perpetrators and the community that such hate violence would not be tolerated and that San Francisco was united in stamping out the signs of racism. The cleanup day succeeded in its goals of removing the swastikas from public view, giving the community a chance to directly demonstrate its commitment to fighting hate crimes, and bringing together diverse communities for a day to take a joint stand against hate crimes.

However, even while the cleanup day removed the physical vestiges of racism, it remains questionable how successfully it addressed the attitudes that led up to the acts of hate vandalism. For in solving the problem as one of vandalism, the effort failed to acknowledge that the swastikas were reflective of ideas and beliefs held much closer to heart in the community. The focus upon the physical element of the hate crime overlooked the intangible factors of prejudice and racial tensions that had created an environment conducive to the swastikas.

On the other hand, it could be said that the lesson to be learned was in the bringing together of diverse communities to tackle a common goal, that the volunteer physical labor itself was a symbol of the community coming together to fight anti-Asian violence. No doubt, a major part of this effort was intended to impress upon the individual merchants that they were a part of the community and in times of crisis they could rely upon the community to come to their assistance.

But again, the focus upon these individual store owners was perhaps misplaced in that many of them were unaware of the historical and genocidal significance of the swastikas. Given their political naïveté, it is debatable whether they were truly the victims of a hate crime and whether they could appreciate the reasons for the volunteer response. One store owner commented to me that the cleanup was a great gesture, but asked why they hadn't come out before to clean up the general vandalism and whether they would come out when the storefronts were defaced again the following week.

Certainly, the store owners were economically and physically the victims of vandalism, but were they also the victims of a hate crime if some of them failed to understand the intended racist message of the perpetrator(s)? Given that several did not understand the import of the symbols, was it critical for the people and politicians to rally behind them in a show of community support?

According to the traditional principles of criminal law and specifically the law around hate crimes, these store owners are the victims of a hate crime. Generally, the definition of a hate crime turns on the intent of the perpetrator and not the understanding of the victim. For example, many jurisdictions hold that a man who is attacked because he is *perceived* to be gay—even if he is not in fact gay—would be the victim of a hate crime, and the perpetrator could be subject to enhanced penalties. On the other hand, a person who fights with a gay person motivated solely by a dispute over a parking space would not be subject to hate-crime penalties even if the gay person was subjectively afraid that the dispute was over his sexual orientation. This follows the general principles of criminal law, which focus on the heart and intent of the perpetrator.

However, what makes hate crimes punishable above and beyond the physical act of criminality is the recognition that hate violence carries levels of psychological and emotional impact well beyond the simple commission of the crime. The penalties for hate crimes are more severe because we recognize that based upon a history of racial intolerance the victims are particularly vulnerable and suffer levels of injuries far beyond the physical and objective damages. Burning a cross on the lawn of an African American is much more than an act of arson or vandalism; it carries with it the clear threat of further escalation of violence when considered in the context of historical precedent.

Thus, when the victim fails to understand or is unaware of the message of hate, much of the psychological trauma and venom of the crime is not present, and from the individual victim's viewpoint it becomes virtually indistinguishable from a simple act of vandalism. Interestingly enough, several of the store owners indicated that they were unaware of the swastikas or the meanings of the swastikas until after the police and media explained to them the significance behind the symbol. Then they became truly afraid and intimidated.

So, should some of the store owners who did understand the message of intimidation and racial hatred and who suffered the psychological consequences be considered victims of hate violence, while the other store owners are not? Should the White karate-store owner whose store was defaced be considered a victim of anti-Asian violence? Were some of the merchants not victims until after they were briefed by the media or police?

Clearly, the focus on the individual level makes little sense, because the bottom line is that property-based hate crimes such as these are clearly an attack upon the community. Common sense dictates that, given the swastika's symbolism of racial hatred and violence, its use defines the incident as one of hate violence, regardless of the understanding of the owner of the property. But if the merchants were not particularly intimidated by this act, then was the cleanup perhaps for the benefit of the community, as opposed to assisting these particular individuals? After all, the older, predominantly Jewish neighborhood was certainly put on notice—in a manner similar to the effects of a cross-burning—once the swastikas were carved into their community's stores.

A more cynical and jaded viewpoint would be that the cleanup was not directed at helping the Asian American merchants at all but rather only at the larger Jewish community, which had to be confronted with the swastikas every day.

The Neighborhood and Geographic Community As Victims?

A second Asian American county supervisor organized two town-hall meetings to facilitate discussions on the placement of swastikas in the community. The events were advertised in several languages to both the Asian merchants and the Sunset community at large. I and several other Chinese-speaking volunteers conducted special outreach to the merchants along the Irving corridor in an attempt to encourage their participation in the hearings. A non-Asian leader in hate-crime coalition work was selected to lead the discussions, and hate-crime "experts," police, elected officials, media, and community groups were invited to attend.

Nearly two hundred people attended the first town-hall meeting, but virtually none of the Asian victim-merchants attended either of the sessions. The discussions were mostly dominated by a number of neighborhood conservation and watch groups from the Sunset—many of whom were involved and continued to be involved in the efforts to drive the Burger King out of the Sunset District.

The first forum was opened with statements of support from local elected officials and presentations by the hate-crimes experts. However, as the discussions progressed and the floor was opened up to those in attendance, the talk quickly turned to combating vandalism generally in the community and the changing character of the neighborhood. "Changing character of the neighborhood," of course, was a euphemism for the rapid growth of the Asian American community in the Sunset—some say at the expense of the older Jewish Russian community. More neighborhood watch groups and closer cooperation with the police were proposed, and a vandalism task force and hot line were discussed. After the opening few minutes, the discussion of "hate" had been dropped and the audience spoke only of the "crimes."

In a more disturbing segment of the town-hall meeting, audience members testified that the real problem contributing to the rise in crime was the fact that the community had changed so much that they didn't feel that this was their community anymore. Asian-language signs dominated the streets and you couldn't even hear English spoken anymore. These "new" residents packed too many family members to a household, didn't try to assimilate, hung out only with their own, did not participate in the civic affairs of the community, and did not fit into the Sunset character.

In an ironic twist, several residents complained that the merchants were at fault for not acting quickly to eradicate the swastikas once they appeared. (Can an Asian merchant be guilty of abetting the commission of a hate crime if he or she refuses to remove a swastika on his or her window in a predominantly Jewish neighborhood?) These residents stated that they were offended that the stores did not act responsibly and rapidly to remove the signs of hate once they were carved on their front windowpanes. The residents who appeared at this public forum indicated that the problem was that the Asians did not participate in the neighborhood watches and other civic duties of the "community," and thus hate crimes and vandalism were allowed to flourish. In a loosely controlled forum, the audience had come full circle in scapegoating the victims as the perpetrators. These were the voices and faces heard that night on the eleven o'clock news.

One resident in particular, who was prominently featured during the media coverage of the community forums as a neighborhood leader, was widely regarded among the Asian American merchants as the leader of the racist and exclusionary forces against them. He had months earlier led the campaign against the Burger King and said to the owner of the Burger King, "We don't want your cheap, sleazy, *yellow* sign here in the Sunset" (emphasis added).

It should be noted that this was as much a case of ethnic conflict as it was a dispute between old-timers and newcomers. Some of those who spoke out against the transformation of the neighborhood included established Japanese Americans who also could not read the Chinese-language signs or understand the foreign languages being spoken on the street.

When I spoke earlier with the Asian American merchants, they expressed a general disinterest in attending such a forum and noted that the scheduled times conflicted with their business hours. I tried everything from pleading with their sense of community to challenging their ethnic pride to pitching it as a smart business decision why they should attend the sessions. But I think the true reason why many failed to attend was a premonition that their issues, concerns, and needs would remain unaddressed in this public setting. Perhaps they thought they would be unable to communicate the depth of their hopes and fears through an interpreter. Many expressed a fear of becoming involved and subjecting themselves to potential future retaliation. And maybe they already knew who their neighbors were and didn't want to walk into a hostile trap.

In trying to open up discussions with the community, officials had allowed the content of the discourse to shift without moderation and thereby granted legitimacy and press to a particular viewpoint of the community. In empowering a certain segment of the community that was hostile to the "Asian invasion" of their community, the town-hall meetings served to further divide and separate the community. Sometime between the first and second town-hall meetings, several businesses owned by non-Asians displayed signs calling for "No hate crimes in the Sunset, except against Burger King."

All of a sudden, it became clear "who killed Vincent Chin." The community leaders who had turned out ostensibly to combat hate crimes were in fact perpetuating many of the same hate-filled messages in their own homes. No doubt it was some juvenile who committed the physical act of vandalism, but the hate was being taught at home.

The town-hall meetings ended after the second forum. Nothing ever came of them.

The California Public As Victims?

The final response from the government involved a state-assembly member who proposed legislation nearly a year later that would elevate hate crimes to a "wobbler" offense, allowing prosecutors the discretion to charge perpetrators with either a misdemeanor or a felony depending on the seriousness of the offense. In doing so, he cited the growing increase in hate crimes in general and the swastikas in the Sunset in particular.

The legislator also pulled together a press conference involving leaders of the Asian Pacific American community and other hate-crime professionals. The press conference was designed to send a message to the community that hate crimes would be prosecuted seriously and the offender subject to felony imprisonment.

The proposed legislation passed. It arguably carries some deterrence value to the extent that it will generate a degree of publicity by having a public official condemn the commission of hate crimes. However, it is unlikely to bear much impact, given that only a small fraction of hate crimes are ever solved by the police and an even smaller fraction of that number are ever prosecuted as hate crimes. In San Francisco, where a hate-crime investigations unit actually exists within the police department and a hate-crime prosecutions unit exists within the district attorney's office, out of more than three hundred hate crimes reported in 1997 to the police unit, there were only thirteen arrests referred to the district attorney's office, with an annual total of only seven convictions for hate crimes, six of which resulted from a plea bargain.

While the passage of hate-crime legislation might deter the commission of a hate crime in the future by increasing the penalty, even if the perpetrators had been arrested in the Sunset District case, their imprisonment would do nothing to address the underlying tensions within the community.

The Asian Pacific American Community As Victims?

The underlying issue remains that the swastikas were only a symptom of a deeper-rooted problem and not the issue in and of themselves. This constituted neither a juvenile prank nor a simple act of vandalism but rather a powerful symbol of communities in conflict and a visible mark of the underlying tensions around a changing demographic in the Sunset District.

No doubt the commission of the hate vandalism in this case was a juvenile act; however, the intent behind the swastikas was not a childish thought but one shared by a large segment of the community: you are threatening the integrity and character of the neighborhood, you must be marked and destroyed. And in the town-hall discussions, while many residents repudiated the specific act of carving swastikas on business storefronts, no one spoke against the underlying message of racial intolerance and disharmony.

Anti-Asian violence results from the friction generated by two communities beginning to rub against each other where no discussion or relationship exists between the communities. Because we are perceived as new, because we are seen as foreign, we are interpreted as a threat. The 1996 national audit on anti-Asian violence prepared by the National Asian Pacific American Legal Consortium and the Asian Law Caucus documents an increase in hate crimes in housing projects, in the political arena, in schools, and in these emerging Asian communities. As our community continues to grow, we can only expect to see a greater incidence of hate violence directed against us. Viewing this situation in a historical context, what happened in the Sunset District was identical to what has happened in countless other cities, such as Monterey Park in Southern California or Queens in New York, where a fast-growing Asian American immigrant population began to "threaten" the character of an "older" neighborhood. As in an earthquake, the shifting and overlapping plates build up increasing resentment until there is a sudden release in the form of a hate crime.

CONCLUSION

Asian Americans are made, not born (or naturalized), and anti-Asian violence is the pain prefacing the light that delivers them into our community. It is a recognition not only that you share a common bond and experience with all other Asians Americans based upon your experiences here in the United States, but that based upon the bond you have an obligation to act on behalf of the community. The Asian American identity is based in part upon an understanding that anti-Asian violence has played an integral part in the history of both America and Asian America and that it has always served to exclude and deny us our rightful place. Asian America lives in the struggle for recognition and existence, and by combating anti-Asian violence we fight the message that we do not belong, that we have no place in America. It is a recognition that the attack upon the individual is an attempt to silence us all, and therefore to break our silence we must speak up for the individual. Thus, while the community may be defined by isolation and exclusion from the mainstream, it is also created from the response to anti-Asian violence, from the organizing.

But more than being defined by exclusion, the achieving of community includes a recognition that Asian America lives in the heart. The history of Asian Americans is the history of the struggle for recognition and equality. Our forefathers and foremothers planted seeds in the cracks of mountains as they planted dynamite high above the railroads in the deserts of Wyoming, as they survived the concentration camps of Arizona, crossed the oceans on flotsam and refugee boats, parachuted in from modern jets, and seared in the fires of Koreatown. The acres of history that we have tilled have been neither welcoming nor fertile, but we have persevered, and out of the desert we have taken seed and we have grown. The promise of America is not happiness or equality but the pursuit of happiness and the opportunity to advocate for equality. In order for us to be recognized as equals, we must struggle to assert our right to sit at the table.

3

Hate Crime on the Internet: The University of California, Irvine, Case

Mavis K. Lee

THE CRIME

On September 20, 1996, Asian American students at the University of California in Irvine, California, received the following e-mail[1]:

> From: "Mother Fucker (Hates Asians)" <mfucker@uci.edu>
> Subject: FUck You Asian Shit
>
> Hey Stupid fucker
> As you can see in the name, I hate Asians, including you. If it weren't for asias at UCI, it would be a much more popular campus. You are responsible for ALL the crimes that occur on campus. YOU are responsible for the campus being all dirt. YOU ARE RESPONSIBLE. That's why I want you and your stupid ass comrades to get the fuck out of UCI. IF you don't I will hunt all of you down and Kill your stupid asses. Do you hear me? I personally will make it my life career to find and kill everyone one of you personally. OK?????? That's how determined I am.
> Get the fuck out,
> MOther FUcker (Asian Hater)

Approximately sixty members of the Asian American community at UC Irvine received this terrifying and demeaning message threatening their lives.

67

The e-mail was sent by a nineteen-year-old named Richard Machado, a former student at UC Irvine, who had been expelled for poor academic performance. Mr. Machado sent this death threat targeting Asian students because he does not like Asians, he believes there are too many Asians at UC Irvine, and he thinks Asians "lower the prestige" of the campus. He believes Asians are responsible for all the crimes that occur on campus and that they make the campus a dirty place. He believes they are "too smart," "study too hard," "get good grades," "raise the curve," and "make it harder for non-Asians to compete." So he composed the message, disguising his true identity, and sent it out to scare his victims.

The scene of the crime was the computer lab at the Engineering Gateway Building on the UC Irvine campus. On the morning of September 20, Mr. Machado logged on to the computing system at the Office of Academic Computing using an alias. He selected the victims of his intended threat by using a program that enabled him to see who was logged on to the computing system of UC Irvine at the same time he was and by choosing e-mail addresses that appeared to belong to Asians, e.g., *mwong@uci.edu, cpark@uci.edu,* and *pnguyen@uci.edu.* He first sent a test message to himself, *rmachado@uci.edu,* to verify that his alias, *mfucker@uci.edu,* in fact worked. He then selected and typed in the e-mail address of each of the targeted recipients, including his own true e-mail address. He sent the message the first time at 10:54 A.M. He waited several minutes for a response. Receiving none, he assumed the e-mail had not transmitted and decided to send it again. He logged out of the terminal he was working on, went to a different terminal in the same computer lab, logged on, and composed and sent the identical message a second time to the same victims. After he sent the hate mail a second time, a flood of responses began to pour in. Recipients replied to the sender and to other victims with a range of reactions from anger, to fear, paranoia, and disbelief.

> To all who are offended,
>   Let not this "Mother Fucker" get away with this nonsense. I am behind you all the way!
>   I'm sick of stupid punks like this, I already ran into racism during my senior year in hs [high school], and I'm f*cking SICK OF

IT!!@! . . . If the guy or gal is CAUGHT, THE NAME SHOULD BE RELEASED, since it [would] be only fair to us all.

First of all I would like to state that I am not Asian, yet I am tremendously disturbed by this hate mail. I hope action is taken to find who wrote this, and the proper discipline is employed. If not, I will have to take this e-mail through the proper administrative channels. Thank you for your time concerning this matter.

Hey guys,

Whatever you guys want to do with this "uneducated fool," i am in. I think that we should not tolerate this type of behavior at UCI campus. Obviously, the person used port 25 to send anonymous mail. I think the root at uci can trace this guy out easily. I'll forward all the hate mails to every dean on campus. I'll try my best to dig this guy out, and I'll let you guys know more about it.

Hey fellas—Its pretty messed up this person who sent us e-mail has penetrated into the system to divulge his views. I for one would love to meet this person so i can teach them a lesson. I really don't know what to think of this letter since I've never gotten one, but what do you guys propose to do? This matter should not be taken lightly . . . especially this day and age. Feel free to write back.

Hi all,

I am a UCI staff member who just read my mail. I was just [as] shocked as the rest of you and I showed it to the Assistant Vice Chancellor, who works in the same office as I do. He is outraged as well. He requested a copy of the hate mail (which is now sitting on his desk) and I know he WILL expose this incident. Keep me posted, folks.

Upon seeing these reactions, Mr. Machado fueled the anger and fear of the recipients with a third e-mail. This time, he used his real name, sent it from his real e-mail account, and pretended that he too was an innocent victim of the hateful e-mail. He said, referring to the sender of the hate mail,

The person thought [I] was asian. Pretty dumb guy. It's obvious he faked his user id somehow to write this message so it will be pretty hard to find him. Just keep an eye out for any suspicious people.
Signed, Richard Machado

Contrary to Mr. Machado's assertion, it was not hard to find him. In fact, at the time he was composing and sending the hate mail, one of the recipients of the e-mail, Jason, who was a student employee of the Office of Academic Computing, from where Mr. Machado sent the hate mail, was upstairs in the same lab working. From the header information in the e-mail, Jason was able to identify the location of the terminal used to send the e-mail. He realized that the sender was sitting in the same building and the same lab he was in. He went downstairs to the terminal to see if the culprit was there. By the time Jason got downstairs, Mr. Machado had moved on to the second terminal to send the second message. Jason went back upstairs to his desk. A few minutes later, Jason received the second hate mail. He went downstairs again to see if he could catch the sender in the act. This time, he saw Mr. Machado still sitting at the terminal. Afraid to confront the person behind the threat, Jason notified his immediate supervisor, the director of the computing center. His supervisor spoke to Mr. Machado. Mr. Machado denied doing anything wrong. He was then asked to cease all activity on the computer and leave the lab immediately.

THE INVESTIGATION

The matter was referred to the UC Irvine campus police for criminal investigation. Unbeknownst to Mr. Machado, surveillance cameras in the computer lab videotaped his two hours of criminal activity. The UC Irvine police obtained a copy of the surveillance videotape from the lab. Cross-referencing the date and time on the videotape with the date and time and terminal information in the header of the hate mail conclusively established Mr. Machado's presence at the terminals from where the two threats were sent, at the times they were sent.

On September 28, Mr. Machado was called into the campus police station and asked to talk about the hate-mail incident. During the interview, the investigating officers asked him whether he'd sent the e-mails. At first Mr. Machado denied any wrongdoing. He stated he had only been in the computer lab for five minutes when he was asked to leave. Only after the investigating officer confronted Mr. Machado with the surveillance videotape did Machado admit to sending the e-mails. In a signed written statement, he explained:

On September 20, 1996, at approximately 10 am, I went into OAC to use the computer terminals. I was bored and decided to mess around. I wanted to see people's reaction to an e-mail. I proceeded to type people's addresses into an e-mail letter. I typed a fake user name. I then wrote the body, giving a sense of hatred. But my intentions were not that of [the] letter. I was bored, it was a week before school, and I meant no harm whatsoever. The body [of the message] was against Asians and their involvement on campus. I wrote that they were responsible for all crimes on campus and that I would kill them. I went ahead and sent it. I then left and went to the other room, still in OAC. I checked to see if they received it, they had not. I sent it again. This time e-mail was returning with notification to OAC of the letter. I was on Netscape at that time, around 11 am. At that time, a supervisor walked [up] to me, asked for ID, and told me what had just happened. He then asked me to leave the building. I left at 11:05 or 11:35 am. Once again, my intentions were spontaneous, unrehearsed and with no bad intentions.
—Richard Machado

During the interview with the UC Irvine investigating officer, Mr. Machado further explained he intentionally targeted Asians because he believes Asians are all nerds, there are too many Asians at UC Irvine, they keep the crime up on campus, they make the campus a dirty place, they bring down the image of UC Irvine and they make UC Irvine less prestigious than UCLA.

The UC Irvine police referred the case to the Federal Bureau of Investigation for investigation into a potential hate crime, and the FBI referred the case to the United States Attorney's Office in the Central District of California for prosecution. On November 13, 1996, a federal grand jury returned an indictment against Mr. Machado for violating the civil rights of the recipients of the hate mail, in accordance with Title 18, United States Code, Section 245(b)(2)(A), which covers interference with federally protected activities. In particular, he was charged with using force or the threat of force to willfully injure, intimidate, or interfere with each recipient of the e-mail because of his or her race, color, or national origin and because he or she was attending a public university.

THE PROSECUTION'S CASE

The federal case against Mr. Machado attracted significant media attention in the legal community, the Asian American community, and the cyberspace community nationwide and around the world. In particular, it drew considerable attention from free-speech proponents because the line between protected political speech and illegal threats in cyberspace had not previously been tested in the courts. As the first criminal prosecution of a hate crime on the Internet, it established new legal precedent.

The case first went to trial in Santa Ana, California, in November of 1997. During the trial, the prosecution called ten victims whose testimonies about what it was like to receive such a terrifying and degrading message were representative of the other fifty victims' experiences. The stories of these students—who ranged from first-generation, American-born Chinese Americans, to immigrants who fled Communist Vietnam with their families during the Vietnam War, to third-generation Korean Americans—were revealing.

I was horrified. At first I thought this "Asian-hater" actually knew me, knows how I look like. I was afraid that he would really "hunt me down" . . . I was also scared because I didn't know how he found out my e-mail address. I was also scared because he has easily obtained my e-mail address, and thus could also obtain my address. . . . I kept on thinking about who this person is and if he really knows me. I was scared of going to school on the first day back because I kept having this feeling that he is out there looking.

My initial feeling was that of shock and anger. I couldn't believe that someone could have sent such mail. Then I was confused. I was confused because I was wondering how this person got my e-mail address. . . . Because of getting this hate mail, I had a hard time falling asleep. I kept thinking in my head that if that person was able to get my e-mail address, then they would also have access to much of my personal information as well. Receiving this mail has also caused a lot of stress on my job. . . . Most of my hours that I work are at night and I usually don't get off work until 1:00 a.m., so I was afraid that someone may have tried to jump me or something after I got off from work. . . . Right now, I still have that feeling of uneasiness when I'm at work. Plus, I still have some trouble sleeping at times. And I'm still kind of angry that someone would still be so ignorant as to send this kind of mail.

At beginning I read the letter I think this person is just messing around but after a while I started to think what happens if this person is serious. He can look me up and have my home address. I am currently living at home. Now, I am not worried for my safety but also my family members.

When I logged on, I was blown away. I didn't know what this was regarding, who it was from, and it was very derogatory. It got me really upset. It degrades Asians. It threatens my life, my safety. It intrudes on my privacy. I mean, your phone number's listed . . . your address is out there. I was scared. I was very distracted all day. I didn't get any work done that day. I went home early that day. I didn't have any close friends or families in Orange County. I wanted to go home to my family where I feel safe. I was almost to the state of paranoia because you don't know who to look out for. I just get scared looking at people.

I was very scared. The e-mail made me really scared to a point where I wouldn't even walk alone on campus. My friends would take turns to pick me up from classes because I have late classes. And I bring mace with me when I walk on campus even though there are friends with me.

This is the first time where someone actually directly e-mailed me a hate mail. While I was reading it sent a chill down my spine, and then later I was angered by the act! E-mail is a tool of convenience; why do people use it otherwise?

First when I received this message I got very angry and mad about it. And after a day or two days, I'm thinking about this mail, and I got intimidated and scared.

The prosecution also called the investigating police officers from UC Irvine. They testified about the defendant's written and verbal confession and about the surveillance videotape that captured the defendant's actions the morning of September 20. Prosecutors also called the personnel of the computer lab, who explained how the evidence from the computer logs tied Mr. Machado to the crime.

THE DEFENSE'S CASE

The defense's case revolved around two themes: (1) to elicit sympathy from the jury by establishing Mr. Machado as a sympathetic nineteen-year-old who had come from a disadvantaged background and had overcome many obstacles, and (2) to argue that although the defendant did send the e-mail, he meant no harm; he intended it as a joke, and therefore did not have the specific intent to "willfully injure, intimidate or interfere with the recipient of the e-mail because of his or her race, color or national origin and because he or she was attending a public university"—as would be required for him to be found guilty of the crime charged.

During the defendant's case, Mr. Machado took the witness stand. He testified that he is the youngest of seven children of a close-knit, fatherless family from El Salvador. They currently live in the United States, and he is the only offspring to go to college. He testified that there was tremendous family pride for him and pressure on him to succeed academically and become a medical doctor. Midway through his freshman year at UC Irvine, his eldest brother, his father figure, was murdered in an attempted robbery. The devastating loss of a family member affected his abilities to concentrate at school. It resulted in a spiraling decline in his academic performance, which culminated in his dismissal from school. Because he was ashamed to tell his family of his failure, he pretended to be in school during the remainder of his freshman year and during the first week of what would have been his sophomore year, the same week he sent the e-mail to the Asians. He explained that during the first week of school, he went through the motions of having one of his older brothers drop him off at school, pretending to study, and pretending to go to classes. Instead, he went to the computer lab on campus and surfed the Web. By the end of the week, on Friday, September 20, he was so bored, he just decided to send an e-mail as a joke to get a reaction from people. He never intended to hurt anyone; he never intended to threaten anyone; and he never intended to injure or intimidate anyone, or to interfere with anyone's right to be at UC Irvine.

The defense also called several recipients of the e-mail who stated that they were not personally threatened by the e-mail or did not take it seriously.

THE JURY

The jury, which consisted of nine men and three women, was unable to reach a unanimous decision after three days of deliberations. Accordingly, the judge dismissed the case. Several jurors were interviewed afterward. While most believed that the defendant sent the e-mail and was guilty of the crime charged, they felt sympathetic for the young man. Their comments ranged as follows: "I'm sure he's guilty because of the effort he put into sending the messages, including sending a test message to himself and checking out personal information on the university computer system to select his Asian targets. He clearly knew what he was doing." "[But] it was obvious he was living a lie. He was getting over the murder of his brother. You don't get over that in a day." "It appears this kid has serious mental problems." "What Richard needs is love and care."

THE RETRIAL

After the first trial ended in a mistrial, the United States Attorney's Office decided to retry the case. On January 27, 1998, a new jury of twelve was selected in Orange County. The prosecution's case-in-chief consisted of much of the same evidence. The defense also put on essentially the same case.

During the prosecution's rebuttal case, however, the prosecution called witnesses who had not testified during the first trial. These witnesses painted a darker side of the defendant. In particular, during Mr. Machado's testimony, he swore under oath and under penalty of perjury that he had never before used racially derogatory terms against Asians. However, the prosecution brought in chat-room acquaintances of the defendant from Colorado and South Carolina to testify that he had used racial slurs against Asians during cyber-conversations with them and had threatened Asians in the past. That critical testimony established the defendant as a racist and a liar and significantly undercut the sympathetic picture of him that his attorney had tried to paint.

In addition, the prosecution presented evidence that the UC Irvine police officers had previously investigated an unrelated but similar incident in which Mr. Machado was suspected of sending a threatening e-mail to the campus newspaper staff using a false e-mail address. The officer who investigated that incident testified that she had warned Mr. Machado that sending such an e-mail was not a joke and would be taken seriously by law-enforcement authorities. Thus, contrary to the defendant's testimony, he knew such behavior was not a joke and could involve criminal repercussions.

After two days of deliberations, this jury of eight women and four men returned a guilty verdict. The defendant was subsequently sentenced to one year in federal prison, one year on federal probation, a one-thousand-dollar fine, and mandatory psychiatric counseling.

AFTERMATH

This case was appealed before the United States Court of Appeals for the Ninth Circuit. On September 7, 1999, the appeal was denied and the conviction affirmed.

Since this case, several other cyber-hate-crime prosecutions have resulted in federal criminal convictions (one of which involved a Chinese American student from California Polytechnic University at Pomona who sent a racially derogatory death threat via e-mail to Latino professors and students at California State University, Los Angeles, and other institutions).

NOTE

1. Throughout this chapter, all occurrences of nonstandard capitalization and all errors in usage, spelling, grammar, typing, etc., are reproduced as they appeared in the original e-mails. Corrections (appearing in brackets) have been made only where needed for clarity.

4

$\circledS$

From Vincent Chin to Kuan Chung Kao: Restoring Dignity to Their Lives

Eric Mar

INTRODUCTION

The Granada Hills, California, killing of Filipino immigrant Joseph Ileto on August 10, 1999, was déjà vu to many of us who have been fighting racial violence and hate crimes since the national movement Justice for Vincent Chin began in the early eighties. The quick upsurge of nationwide community actions organized with the leadership of groups like Filipino Civil Rights Advocates (FILCRA), Asian Pacific American Labor Alliance (APALA), and others following Ileto's killing was a reflection of the level of awareness within our communities that had been built over the last two decades, especially within California.

The National Asian Pacific American Legal Consortium (NAPALC) reports that Joseph Ileto was the fifth Asian American killed as a result of anti-Asian violence in 1999. Although the other killings occurred in Indiana, Maryland, and Illinois, the Ileto case is significant because of California's growing Asian and Pacific Islander and immigrant populations. It is no coincidence that many of the attacks on Asian Americans have coincided with the rising wave of anti-immigrant initiatives such as the "English Only" Proposition 63 passed by California voters in 1986, the anti–undocumented immigrant Proposition 187 in 1994, and the anti–bilingual education Proposition 227 in 1998. It

77

is no surprise to many of us in the immigrant-rights movement that the immigrant status of Vincent Chin, Joseph Ileto, and others—or the fact that they "looked foreign"—was an important factor in their killings.

California has undergone a dramatic demographic shift since the passage of the 1965 Immigration Act, which ended a long era of racist exclusion laws against Asians and other people of color. Immigrants, especially from Mexico, Latin America, and Asia, are fueling much of the growth of this new California. Census bureau reports from 1996 show that nearly one in ten people in the United States is foreign born. But in California, over one in five residents is foreign born. The California Research Bureau reports that Asian immigrants make up about one quarter of the state's immigrants, while Latinos make up about half. From 1960 to 1980, the Asian and Pacific Islander population in the state more than quadrupled from less than a third of a million to 1.3 million. The Population Reference Bureau (PRB) estimates that Asians and Pacific Islanders now make up over 3.5 million people in California and are expected to increase to over 6.5 million people by the year 2015. According to the PRB, Latinos will outnumber Whites in California 16.4 million to 15.8 million by that year.

But Paul Ong, Yen Le Espiritu, and other ethnic-studies scholars have also noted that in the decades following the 1965 immigration law, Asian American communities have become more "class polarized," with a growing "professional and managerial class" in addition to the large sectors of our communities locked into low-wage industries or dependent on public assistance. They point out that California's demographic shifts are also occurring in the context of capitalist restructuring on a global scale. The growing disparity between rich and poor, the increasing elimination of U.S. manufacturing-sector jobs, and the expansion of part-time, temporary, and contingent work are all domestic consequences of this process of "corporate globalization," according to anti-WTO (World Trade Organization) labor, environmental, and social-justice activists who organized the massive protests in early 2000 to disrupt the Seattle meeting of the WTO. The impact of this restructuring is increasing California residents' feelings of economic insecurity even in an era of supposed nationwide prosperity—an issue at the heart of the growing resurgence of anti-Asian violence and anti-immigrant scapegoating.

California is experiencing a growing number of "hate crimes" against not just people of color, but also other groups like Jews and lesbian/gay/bisexual and transgender people. Of the two thousand hate crimes reported in California in 1996, only 7.4 percent were committed against Asian Americans. While NA-PALC reported an overall decrease in anti-Asian incidents in their nationwide report in 1997, they noted significant increased reports in California and New Jersey, both states with dramatically changing demographics. Similarly, in multicultural Los Angeles, the Asian Pacific American Legal Center of Southern California found in 1995 that one quarter of the nation's reported anti-Asian incidents occurred in Southern California alone. Karen Umemoto of the University of Hawaii has also noted in her research that hate crimes in Hawaii have been concentrated in areas undergoing demographic changes that typically displace one ethnic or racial group with another.

The San Francisco/Oakland Bay Area, considered one of the most tolerant and "progressive" regions of the country, has been the site of many incidents of anti-Asian and racial violence, especially during the 1980s. During this period, organizations such as Davis Asians for Racial Equality (DARE), Sacramento's Coalition of Asians for Equal Rights (CAER), and the Bay Area's Asian Network for Equality and Justice (ANEJ) formed in direct response to numerous incidents of racial violence against Asians and other people of color in the area. Another, more advocacy-oriented group called Break the Silence Coalition against Anti-Asian Violence (BTS) formed as well after a successful May 1986 conference. At the time, ANEJ and others importantly connected the individual acts of racial violence with a much larger system of institutionalized racism in the United States that serves to "degrade, dehumanize, and reinforce the unequal status" of Asian Americans and other people of color. Some of the leaders also sought to link the fight against anti-Asian violence with a much larger struggle against White supremacy and capitalism in the United States, which they saw as the basic root causes of oppression of Asian and Pacific Islander peoples. While none of these organizations exist today, with the exception of DARE, many of their leaders and members have continued their work through other social-justice community campaigns and organizations.

My personal reflection begins where these activists left off. It chronicles my initial involvement in the Justice for Vincent Chin movement and traces the impact that the April 1997 killing of Chinese immigrant Kuan Chung Kao had on my personal and political lives.

AWAKENING

The funeral of George Lee was an awakening for me. I had never wept publicly before. But my own very powerful feelings, my fifteen years of activism and work against racism and economic injustice, the pride of my community's history of resistance to oppression—all flowed out of me the minute I saw his body lying there motionless in the casket. Partly embarrassed and somewhat relieved about being human after all, I walked by George Lee's body with tears streaming down my face and gave him a symbolic yellow-power salute.

In February 1998, the eighty-five-year-old Mr. Lee died a hero in Chinatown and in the broader tenants'-justice and social-justice movements in San Francisco. He had come to the United States at a very early age and spent most of his adult life working two to three jobs a day to support his family. He and his wife, Chang Jok Lee, had been leaders for decades in the movement for tenant rights and dignity for public-housing residents. With the Ping Yuen Residents Improvement Association (PYRIA) in 1978, Mr. Lee led what has become known as the first "public housing project" rent strike in San Francisco history after the brutal rape and killing of a woman at the Ping Yuen development in Chinatown. PYRIA and its supporters were successful in organizing a bold and courageous four-month strike and in winning many of their twelve demands for improved living conditions and gaining real decision-making power for the Ping Yuen residents and others throughout the city.

In the early seventies, Mr. and Mrs. Lee and others of their generation joined with younger Asian American activists to found the Chinese Progressive Association (CPA), a mass-based people's organization in San Francisco's Chinatown. I have been active in this grassroots organization since 1984. Recently, CPA honored Mr. and Mrs. Lee to loud cheers of respect and love from hundreds of people representing generations of activism in our community. Unfortunately, Mr. Lee had died, of natural causes, the week before he was to receive this honor. But his life will be remembered as one of struggle. He fought the good fight for the building of a better society and for the dignity of all people. The many community people and activists like me that he influenced and touched will never be the same.

I was so profoundly moved by Mr. Lee's death because I knew that he died with dignity and with the respect of his family and community. Kuan Chung Kao had no dignity when he was shot in front of his wife and children by a White police officer in Sonoma County, California, in 1999 and then allowed to die with his hands cuffed behind him, lying face down in the quiet suburban street where he lived.

THE SONOMA COUNTY POLICE KILLING OF KUAN CHUNG KAO

On April 29, 1997, police officer Jack Shields shot and killed thirty-three-year-old engineer Kuan Chung Kao, a Taiwanese immigrant and father of three in the predominantly White middle-class suburb of Rohnert Park, California (about fifty miles north of San Francisco). The sheriff's department and district attorney's offices both found the killing justifiable because Kao had been "brandishing the [broom]stick in a threatening martial-arts fashion." The killing and the blatant racism within the law enforcement agencies and the local media spurred communities throughout northern California to organize for justice for the Kao family, and to call for greater police accountability and an end to racist violence.

The racial stereotypes of Asian people adopted by officials in this case and the attempted justifications for the Kao killing verge on the absurd. The other officer on the scene claimed that Kao was spinning the broomstick like a "ninja fighter." The D.A.'s report included other outrageous comments from neighbors, describing Kao as taking a "Samurai warrior–type stance" before he was killed. Witnesses reported that Shields shot Kao from a distance of about ten to twelve feet. According to Ayling Wu, Kao's widow, he had never studied martial arts. Following the shooting, the police searched the Kao residence in vain for evidence of Mr. Kao's alleged martial-arts expertise.

Reports by police and by the Asian Law Caucus confirm that Kao had been drinking heavily for some seven hours and had a blood alcohol level of 0.23, almost three times the legal limit. Neighbors called 911 after hearing the shirtless and drunk Kao yelling and asking for help. Shields, the second officer to arrive at the scene, shot and killed Kao within seconds of his arrival. As Kao lay dying in his driveway, his wife, a registered nurse, was prevented from administering any emergency medical care for her husband and was threatened with arrest. According to reports, Kao was handcuffed and left face down unattended for eight or nine minutes before the other officer on the scene began any medical treatment. When the ambulance arrived about a minute later, it was too late to save Kao's life.

On June 19, 1997, exactly fifteen years to the day after Vincent Chin was killed in Detroit by being beaten to death with a baseball bat,[1] the Sonoma County district attorney cleared the officers of any criminal charges for Kao's death. The result of the district attorney's investigation is not surprising given that Kao's death was the fourth police-related death in Sonoma County in 1997 and the ninth in two years. In all cases, the district attorney cleared the police of any wrongdoing. Mainstream media reports and local officials were largely influenced from the beginning by the report of the sheriff's investigation, which asserted that Kao assaulted the officer with a "deadly weapon" (the broomstick). The report also failed to acknowledge any of the racism in the incident. In February 1998 the U.S. Department of Justice announced upon completion of its investigation that it would not seek federal civil-rights charges against the police officer because of what it called "a lack of evidence."

OUT OF OPPRESSION ARISES RESISTANCE

My first reaction when I heard of Kao's death through one of my many e-mail lists in early May 1997 was not one of immediate outrage, but instead just a passing thought—"another dead Chinaman." You see, I had become somewhat numbed by the huge string of killings, beatings, and assaults on Asian Americans since Vincent Chin's death in 1982. On June 22, 1997, after reflecting on the Kao case a little more, I cranked out a typical e-mail message to the Asian American and progressive e-mail lists I often "spam" with my rambling thoughts:

On the fifteenth anniversary of Vincent Chin's death: Given the recent "justified" homicide ruling in the Rohnert Park, CA, police killing of Kuan Chung Kao, the racial violence against Southeast Asians in San Francisco public-housing projects, and other increasing incidents across the country, you'd think President Clinton, in his April 14, 1997, speech at UC San Diego on his Initiative on Race, would have mentioned or acknowledged the rise in anti-Asian sentiment and anti-Asian violence.

Instead, Clinton's only mention of Asian Americans was to characterize all of us as "grocers" and to play up "our" tensions with "Black and Latino customers." Don't get me wrong, I think the initiative is important (but so was the Kerner Commission thirty years ago :->). And the appointment of progressive Korean American attorney Angela Oh from Los Angeles to the seven-person task force is a great move. But the last time I remember hearing (a simple) acknowledgement at the national level of anti-Asian violence was during Jesse Jackson's talk about Vincent Chin's killing at the 1984 Democratic National Convention in San Francisco!

Interesting to note that police officer Jack Shields, who killed the thirty-three-year-old Mr. Kao, said that the victim had "brandished a [broom]stick in a threatening martial arts fashion." So he had to shoot him in the chest. And the cops had to prevent Mr. Kao's wife, a nurse, from administering any first aid. And Mr. Kao had to die lying in his own driveway while his wife looked on. The *San Francisco Examiner* reported today that there have been at least five other shooting deaths in Sonoma County (one hour north of SF) since April 1995. . . . Oh, and all of these killings were ruled "justifiable" as well.

Mr. Kao's killing also occurred on the fifth anniversary of the Rodney King uprising. Weird historical parallels. . . . The SF and Sonoma County community groups coming together around the Kao killing are keeping the pressure on. A SF coalition formed last week was pulled together by the Asian Law Caucus. . . . We are planning fundraising, media, and legal support for the family of Mr. Kao and a number of other events. We'll see whether federal civil-rights charges are filed.

Along with a number of other community activists and advocates, I spoke at a June 20, 1997, Justice for Kao press conference
held in San Francisco's city hall. My talk emphasized the importance of the grassroots organizing done during the 1980s by my
group, the Chinese Progressive Association, and many other
progressive groups in the Justice for Vincent Chin movement. I
also repeated a point that Helen Zia, an anti-Asian-violence activist, had made in the Justice for Vincent Chin movement: that
no civil rights case is ever brought to prosecution without community mobilization and organizing.

On August 7, 1997, the newly formed Coalition for Justice for
the Kao Family organized a candlelight vigil at Portsmouth
Square in San Francisco's Chinatown to commemorate the hun-
dredth day after Kao's killing. The hundreds of people in attendance remembered Kao by lighting candles to commemorate his
death. They also witnessed visual images of his life through a
montage of photos of Kao and his family. The vigil proved important by renewing the cry for justice in the case. Prior to the
event, mainstream forces in the coalition actually had opposed
the vigil. It took the foresight and organizing of two of the
younger activists in the coalition—Debbie Ng, an intern at the
Chinese Progressive Association and a student at UC Santa
Cruz, and Michael Chang, an Asian Law Caucus intern and
Ph.D. student at UC Berkeley—to make the vigil happen.

The diverse coalition initiators included leadership from the
Asian Law Caucus, Chinese for Affirmative Action, American
Civil Liberties Union, Organization of Chinese Americans, Chinese Progressive Association, Japanese American Citizens
League, Redwood Empire Chinese Association of Sonoma
County, Bay Area Police Watch, and other groups. From the beginning, many of the grassroots activists, including me, were
wary of getting involved in yet another "united front" effort that
was clearly dominated by lawyers, politicians, and "experts,"
and that limited opportunities for more mass involvement and
progressive action. But we nonetheless helped build the coalition, always promoting the importance of the victim's family's
wishes and their leadership role.

Our second public event was also tremendously successful
and helped build more mass participation in the campaign.
Some one thousand people turned out at the Rally for Justice for

the Kao Family on August 16 in San Francisco's Union Square. The rally was intended to keep public pressure on government authorities for an independent investigation into Mr. Kao's shooting and the subsequent clearing of those involved by the Sonoma County D.A.'s office. The call for justice issued at the rally by Kao's widow, Ms. Wu, for her husband was reminiscent of the courage and strength displayed by Vincent Chin's mother, Mrs. Lily Chin, in the campaign for justice for her son fifteen years earlier. Despite the petty bickering that occurred backstage between local politicians, most of the rally speakers—like young African American activist Van Jones of Bay Area Police Watch—stressed the need for building a "rainbow coalition" against police brutality and for community control of police.

The Union Square rally, notably, included a broader spectrum of groups beyond the usual collection of "professional" activists. The Northern American Guangzhou High School Alumni Association turned out in the hundreds, carrying flowing red-ribbon banners to dramatize the blood shed by victims of racist police violence.

Individual members of the coalition supported other actions. At a rally on October 22 in support of the National Day of Protest against Police Brutality and the Criminalization of a Generation, alongside family members of victims of police violence, I spoke in front of the Stolen Lives Project's huge mock gravestones. The gravestones are engraved with the names and faces of hundreds of victims like Kao. I stressed that Kao's killing must be connected with broader occurrences of legislative and political attacks on immigrants, people of color, and the poor, such as increased INS and border-patrol violence and sweeps, and the devastating impact of welfare "reform" on our communities.

Our work to vindicate Kao's killing seemed to take a positive turn when we learned that the U.S. Commission on Civil Rights was planning formal hearings on the case in northern California. As part of the effort of the Coalition for Justice for the Kao Family, on February 20, 1998, I drove one of several vans full of Chinatown activists and tenant leaders to the hearings called by the U.S. Commission on Civil Rights. Many of the elderly community folks whom we mobilized for the ninety-minute trip to Santa Rosa had worked with the late George Lee on public-housing and social-justice reforms in San Francisco. The Kao coalition was required to provide its own translation equipment and translators for the hearing. Ms. Wu, Kao's widow, was visibly shaken when we arrived to find an intimidating crowd of police officers and their families all wearing yellow ribbons and taking up most of the seats in the tiny auditorium. We were forced, seniors and all, to stand outside the auditorium for hours, and many of us never even made it into the hearing room to witness the bureaucratic drama inside.

The hearings were intended to assist the commission in its investigation of the numerous recent police killings in Sonoma County. The pressure brought to bear by the Kao coalition through community mobilization was a major factor in forcing the commission to come to the Bay Area. Unfortunately, the commission bowed to local police and conservative community pressure and "toned down" its original plans. At the last minute it was decided that instead of a joint forum convened equally by the federal commission and its state advisory committee, all sixteen members of the state advisory committee would actually preside over the meeting, with the federal commission taking a much diminished role. In addition, the commission abruptly reversed its decision to subpoena witnesses after objections from law enforcement officials led to a letter of protest from the Santa Rosa police chief.

Late in the evening, after returning from the hearings and dropping off the last activist, I found myself questioning why I work fifteen-hour days, driving in the pouring rain, trying to speak or give voice to the voiceless, when no one in power seems to be even willing to listen. Were we fooling ourselves to think that by using the methods we had adopted we could stop anti-Asian violence and all hate crimes?

PERSONAL JOURNEY

As a past director of the Northern California Coalition for Immigrant Rights, a nonprofit advocacy group based in San Francisco, I have worked for years to address the day-to-day needs of immigrants and poor and working people. But my other political work outside of my nine to five job often pulls me closer to the kind of real impact I want to make in this world.

My family roots start in Guangzhou, China, and wind through Hawaii and the California Central Valley. My dad is an immigrant from China who settled in the Sacramento Delta area with his family around 1920 when he was a baby. My mom's father was born in Hawaii and settled in Sacramento to raise his family. Mom was born and raised in Sacramento during the Depression. I think her experiences with poverty and racism have given her a special fighting spirit and a unique resourcefulness and practicality that only folks of her generation seem to share. Both of my parents, along with many of my aunts and uncles and cousins, worked for the state of California almost their whole lives. Although my father joined the U.S. Army and fought in World War II, neither he nor my mother had the luxury of a college education. They placed much of their hope for success in me and my brothers and sisters.

Besides my twin brother, Gordon, a longtime activist in the Asian American and environmental-justice movements and executive director of the Chinese Progressive Association, I have four other siblings. One of my sisters was active in the Asian American Political Alliance at UC Berkeley in the late 1960s. My mother and other relatives have historically been active in Asian American community organizations in Sacramento. I am fortunate to have grown up in an environment where community service was so highly regarded. But my family and cloistered surroundings in Sacramento also sheltered me from the blatant racism and exploitation around me.

It wasn't until the early 1980s, after Vincent Chin's killing, that my racial and class identity really hit me. In the midst of the so-called Ronald Reagan revolution, the 1982 Chin killing sparked a nationwide campaign for justice that drew connections between racial violence and the era's pro-corporate, trickle-down economic policies and fanatical anticommunism. Importantly, the community organizing and mobilizing that came out of the movement greatly influenced a new generation of community activists like me.

The classes in Asian American studies and ethnic studies I took as a student at UC Davis formed the beginning of my "political life." About a year after Vincent Chin's death, Davis High School student Thong Huynh was stabbed to death by a group of White youth that had been taunting him with racial slurs.

During classroom discussions of Huynh's killing in my first Asian American studies class, in the fall of 1983, I was able for the first time to talk collectively with other Asian Americans about issues of concern to our community. I later joined Davis Asians for Racial Equality (DARE), a community group that was formed to address the growing anti-Asian sentiment in the area. Angela Oh, one of the members of President Clinton's Initiative on Race, was a founder of DARE, along with other law students, undergraduates (like me), and community members.

I later became active in many other struggles—covering issues from Asian American student and educational rights to fighting anti-immigrant laws and policies and the "English Only" movement. I also developed internationalist politics through my work in the antiapartheid and Central American solidarity movements and in my stint as the editor of *Third World*, a student newspaper on campus.

In my studies I grew fascinated with our country's racist history of immigration and exclusion laws targeted at Asian peoples and with the interconnections between labor and foreign policies. My two mentors at UC Davis, Professors George Kagiwada and Isao Fujimoto, helped me make the link between academic study and my role in the Asian American community and the broader society. They taught me to understand through integration of theory and practice the importance of grassroots community empowerment in any effort to address anti-Asian violence or racial oppression in general. Through their teaching I was ingrained with the principle, now popularized by UCLA scholar/activist Glenn Omatsu, that "knowledge is too important to stay in the classroom."

Today, more than fifteen years later, both Kagiwada and Fujimoto have retired. And I have been teaching at the predominantly working-class San Francisco State University since 1992. My students in the evening courses I teach in Asian American studies and ethnic studies give me hope for the future. We dialogue about the meaning of the 1992 Rodney King uprisings in connection to the 1965 Watts rebellion. We compare the president's Initiative on Race today with the Kerner Commission Report in 1968. We discuss anti-Asian violence in the broader context of our country's history of racial oppression and its class exploitation of Third World peoples.

When we collectively view Christine Choy and Renee Tajima's classic documentary *Who Killed Vincent Chin?*, it is the students who connect Kuan Chung Kao's killing to the unprecedented domestic and worldwide economic changes caused by corporate globalization—including the elimination of our society's safety net, the ongoing downsizing of our workforce, and the constant pitting of workers and communities against each other to fight over crumbs thrown out by the transnational corporations.

Importantly, my students also see right through the shallow "liberal" approaches to eliminating hate crimes promoted by many of our politicians and self-proclaimed community leaders. My students' proposed solutions are decidedly more radical. They emphasize the importance of addressing root causes of racial violence and of promoting strategies like grassroots community organizing and building multiracial coalitions with other people of color and progressive movements. They talk about the "long-term struggle" and are very skeptical of strategies for community "empowerment" that focus solely on electoral and individual economic advancement, because they understand the inherent inequality and deep corruption of our existing political system.

I have tried to give my students at San Francisco State the same opportunity that my teachers gave me: to learn in a supportive environment through practical work about their key role in our community's progress and development. But ultimately, I benefit from our interactions as well, for their hopefulness and idealism help inspire me and keep me going in this difficult political period for immigrants, people of color, and the poor and working classes.

TOWARD LIVES OF DIGNITY

A few months after I learned of Kuan Chung Kao's killing, I saw a picture of the twin baby boys and the six-year-old daughter he left behind. I wondered what their mother, Ayling Wu, would say to her children as they grew up to help them understand the meaning of the racist killing of their father. Would she raise them as my mother has raised my twin brother and me: to stand up for what is right and just? Would she turn the death of her husband into the birth of hope and struggle in her twins and daughter?

Few of us are fortunate to live a life of dignity like that led by Chinatown housing-movement leader George Lee. That is why I am moved to tears by the incredible moments, such as his funeral, when our heroes pass their legacy to those of us willing to carry on their struggles, their dreams of a better world. George Lee passed his torch to many of us who remember his life. I have hope that we can turn Kuan Chung Kao's and Vincent Chin's lives from tragedies into lives of dignity, like George Lee's, through our work to organize, educate, and empower our communities.

NOTE

1. Vincent Chin was a twenty-seven-year-old Chinese immigrant draftsman and waiter who was killed a week before his wedding by two White, laid-off Chrysler autoworkers who thought Chin was Japanese and blamed him for the decline in the U.S. auto industry. Nine months later, in March 1983, the killers pleaded guilty; they received three years of probation and were fined $3,780.

II

❀

LANGUAGE AND
IDENTITY

5

Some Substitute Stories, Out of School

Ashok Mathur

A WORD BEFORE

The stories that follow are sometimes more reflections than fictions; sometimes, the other way around. Much of this interrupting narrative flows around the critical text, rather than preceding or proceeding in linear fashion. This process is intended to create a sense of simultaneity such that the text (and here I mean the entire body of words and language encompassed in this article) challenges a readership and writership with the effect of creating a stronger sociopolitical reading. I want to point to the tenuous nature of this flowaround text, which resists the common effect of glossing or footnoting, which renders one reading subordinate to another (or at least to tertiary importance). In the associated text below, I have tried to move, obviously not seamlessly, between an analysis of story through to story and back through a further analysis. What I hope to accomplish is a reading of these stories/anecdotes/critiques that does not place more credence on either storytelling or critically analytical modes. The stories are about a form of violence, about how language and its components can comprise a type of sustained, systemic assault. As critical race theorists Charles Lawrence III, Mari Matsuda, Richard Delgado, and Kimberlè Williams Crenshaw point out in *Words That Wound*, the violence of hate speech can and does inflict injury not dissimilar, legally or otherwise, to a physical assault. And while Judith Butler argues that the state in effect *creates* hate speech through its very ratification of the category, I suggest that outside the realm of jurisprudence, hate*ful* speech has pernicious power and the ability to regulate the constructions of racial (and other forms of) identity. I will begin, then, by briefly addressing the concept of self-naming through the work of a Sri Lankan Canadian poet and move from there through a series of anecdotes and analyses.

WORDS FROM AN EPIC POEM

In 1997 Toronto-based writer and activist Krisantha Sri Bhaggiyadatta self-published a chapbook titled *Aay, Wha' Kinda Indian Arr U?* through which the narrative voice interrogates itself line after line in an attempt to answer the question posed by the title. This politics of naming is, of course, crucial in any project around identity, but the question of *who* is doing the naming is equally important. In Bhaggiyadatta's text, the "I" of the poem constantly questions itself: "am I a near Indian or a far Indian or a very very much lost Indian or 'jes Indian, / an eas'Indian or a wes'Indian eas'Indian or the central Indian in a cast of outcastes in a chapaati-western movie" (1), calling into question the social history of Indianness as it has come to represent peoples from the South Asian diaspora and beyond. Bhaggiyadatta is able to move from the general —"am I . . . an Indo-Canadian Indian"— to the specific—"am I Preeti Wadedar, she, who died leading the attack on the Railway Officer's Club in 1932" (1)—causing the reader to reflect on what it means to adopt a community name or an individual name, both of which occupy particular places in history. But such a process is articulated by Bhaggiyadatta as a self-naming, a calling of oneself into being through enunciating a name by which *others* might call the self. In doing so, Bhaggiyadatta's poem weaves a story of naming through history, but the reader is constantly reminded of the explicit "am I" that precedes the various "kinds" of *Indian*. This pair of words, prefixed to what amounts to a series of more than two hundred "kinds," has the effect of (1) prefacing the first-person singular in all the questions posed and (2) setting up a strategy of rhetorical question, for it becomes apparent that the querying "I" is not asking this list of questions with any expectation of a response. I point this out because Bhaggiyadatta's work, which he calls an epic poem, manages to call into question the role agents of colonialism, imperialism, capitalism, and white supremacy play in the naming (and subjugating) of the racialized subject *without* removing power from the acting subject (i.e., the subject who asks, "am I?"). As such, *Aay, Wha' Kinda Indian Arr U?* acts as a powerful critique of the social, political, and economic histories affecting peoples of the South Asian diaspora and others who are subjected to these histories.

WORDS THAT NAME OURSELVES

However, the act of self-naming becomes embattled when, as is usually the case, the individual subject is disallowed the privilege of naming herself or himself from within a known social sphere and is instead quite literally *made* or brought into being by a naming from elsewhere. In the following story (and in stories two and three to some degree) I try to point to the re-articulation of self-naming in various capacities. I will start with the obvious, that the act of naming is a method of recollecting shared knowledge through language. On a simple semiotic level, then, when I utter a word such as "man," it conjures up a mental image and/or some concept for others who share my language structure. The concept of "man" conjured up by my friend may differ from my concept of "man," but, depending on our language base and cultural similarities, there will be some such entity that we both agree upon to be signified by the word "man." I belabor this point to illustrate the types of naming and name-calling that occur in the following story. I argue that what occurs is an *interpellation* of the subject, in that "ideology 'acts' or 'functions' in such a way that it 'recruits' subjects among the individuals . . . by that very precise operation which [Althusser calls] interpellation or hailing, and which can be imagined along the lines of the most commonplace everyday police (or other) hailing: 'Hey, you there!'" (Althusser 144).

My critique, my "reading" of this story comes before and after the "telling" of the story, so that the story is prefaced and post-scripted with this commentary and, I hope, integrated into this analysis. At first, the "substitute" (that is, one who "stands in for the 'real'") interpellates me as a "troublemaker." Important to recognize, but not "named" by me in this story, is the implicit power structure of teacher to student, although this is compli-cated by the fact that this particular teacher is "standing in" and this particular student "stands in" in a different way for the teacher. At any rate, also implicit are the race relations: the teacher is white, the student is brown. Being an unknown quan-tity (as are the rest of the students) to this particular substitute teacher, the student in question is brought into being for her as a troublemaker, that is, someone who requires *particular* attention, someone whom the teacher will "keep an eye on." But fore-grounding this knowledge is the instance of race. A quick scan of the classroom by the substitute will establish the racial demo-graphics of the classroom, namely that this is an all-white sub-urban class—all white save for one. Critical pedagogy research (and even standard studies of education and race) informs us that there is a *tendency* for white teachers to target students of color as less intelligent, less able, and more trouble than their white counterparts. I would argue, incidentally, that race works in this case to *single out* students of color, to focus on them un-naturally, sometimes in a manner that is correctly named as "benevolent" racism, that is, the tendency for white teachers to remark upon favorably or otherwise denote the performance of a student of color in an overcompensation for assumptions such as are stated above. I move into the first "substitute story" then, and will comment on it more afterward.

STORY ONE: Ashok, in grade seven, is not by any means a trou-blemaker or even, at least by that time, a class clown. He sits dur-ing homeroom in his assigned seat (fourth from the front) in his assigned row (furthest to the right, by the door), and a substitute teacher walks in. She looks stern. She frowns. She glares at the students. Lesson begins. She asks them what their regular teacher had planned for them, what they were reading, that sort of thing. A student volunteers some information. Someone else adds to that, embellishing it somewhat. Somewhere in the recesses of his mind, Ashok remembers something their homeroom teacher had told them they would be doing today, and Ashok volunteers that information. Don't forget, this is grade seven, a roomful of pubescent boys and girls, and this is a substitute teacher, the ultimate permission for even the best child to act his or her worst. So Ashok supposes he somewhat embellishes his story, too, yet, not too good at lying, Ashok grins ear to ear when he tells her what their regular teacher had planned for them today. The substitute teacher frowns further, determines there could not possibly be an element of truth to what Ashok is saying (which is, of course, not true) and then points an accusatory finger at him: "I'm going to be keeping an eye on *you*," she says. The class thinks this is hilarious. Ashok normally speaks only when spoken too and has, in all likelihood, never been reprimanded in his school life. The substitute teacher's finger wags slightly as she continues to point. "What is your name?" she demands. The class laughs even harder. Ashok looks around. Ashok swallows. "Jim," Ashok says still smiling. "My name is Jim." And the class continues to laugh, this time at his obvious lie, but the sub dismisses this as simple childish classroom behavior and goes on about the business of her lesson plan.

To be interpellated as someone who requires an authority figure to either "finger" one or to watch over one excessively is to be hailed as someone worthy of such an intense gaze. But what happens when that interpellated subject re-interpellates himself? In this story, Ashok renames himself as "Jim," an act of defiance toward a (substitute) authority, taking a Christian name—perhaps not with willful intention, but nonetheless, taking a name derived from a version of the Bible itself—to supplant a Buddhist-cum-Hindu name. More simply put, Ashok takes on a name that is at once more familiar to the teacher's repertoire of names *and* more unfamiliar in that such a moniker has no history in attachment to Ashok's sense of self. In Shani Mootoo's novel *Cereus Blooms at Night*, a Christian missionary's desire to rename his Hindu student is met with open reception by the student, who wants to shed all indicators of his past identity. Similarly, I think, Ashok's utterance self-interpellates him, brings him into being as "Jim," and, thus named, he becomes somehow less brown under the gaze of the substitute teacher. Arguably, such a defiance is a self-protective gesture, beating the authority figure to the punch, so to speak, saying "I can bring myself into your (white) world by uttering myself as such." Such a renaming of the self also deflects the violent insistence of the teacher that she will wield complete control through the suggestion of a panoptic gaze by disallowing her full access to Ashok—that is, by withholding his name, he gets to keep some of himself from the aggressive control of the teacher. I will not go so far as to suggest that such self-naming does indeed resituate the subject's racial position, because this is complicated by numerous factors, but I want to end this commentary on the following note: the brown gaze implicitly described in this story, that of Ashok receiving the finger-pointing from a white pedagogical authority, is met with an escapist lie. Ashok does not truly rename himself, neither thinks nor wishes himself as Jim, but utters this name as a facade, as a trick to deceive what he perceives as a particularly unfair threat based on preconceived notions of race and identity.

WORDS FROM WHITE FOLKS

The second story consists of two important components: first, how the brown student reacts to the appearance of a South Asian substitute teacher; second, how the colleagues of this brown student articulate their perceptions of race through associative valuing. In the first instance, the brown student notices, presumably as do his costudents, the *differences* between the "regular" teacher and the substitute. Most important are the racial differences—the substitute is immediately racialized, thought of as *brown* or *East Indian* or in some unnamed form *nonwhite*. Important to this train of thought is that the regular, or perhaps I should say *normal*, teacher is not brought into being as a white man *until* a brown man stands in for him. This occurs, again in varying degrees, for both the brown student and his white colleagues, an indication that people of color in a white-supremacist society are also quite susceptible to normalizing whiteness and distinguishing race as something somehow possessed or "worn" by nonwhites. In this case, the very appearance of the South Asian substitute creates a fear of self-awareness for the South Asian student. He is afraid other students are turning to *him* as some sort of extension of the substitute, occasioned by the two of them simply *being* brown in a white realm. Further, the brown student hopes beyond hope that the South Asian substitute will not differentiate himself further from whiteness by marking himself with an accent that is recognized as *other*, which, curiously, marks him as closer to the "type" of brown person the brown student wishes *not* to be identified with. But the South Asian substitute *does* speak with an accent and does occasion a certain form of derision from the class.

STORY TWO: Scoot ahead three years, from the first year of junior high to the first year of senior high. Grade ten, chemistry class. One day, their aging and somewhat crotchety chem teacher doesn't shuffle through the doors of the lab and make his way up to the front of the class. Instead, there is a replacement teacher, a substitute, resembling their regular teacher only in gender. The substitute is some years younger than the regular teacher. And he is dressed somewhat snappier, not in the absent-minded, inside-out professorial clothes of the regular teacher. And he is brown. Not just any brown, but South Asian–brown, or as Ashok thinks at the time, Indian–brown, me–brown. In his designated seat in his designated row he shrinks down from an already diminutive-for-high-school size. Ashok imagines (or does he?) that a dozen sets of eyes taking in their new substitute turn to take him in. The substitute begins to speak. He speaks—*oh let him sound like our regular teacher, don't let him have . . .*—with an accent. All ears attune to the substitute's accent and then, Ashok imagines (?), immediately attune to the way *he's* supposed to speak. During the substitute's first few utterances Ashok thinks of all the times he's scurried his friends through his home lest they meet up with and hear accented extended family. So un-Canadian. And so the class goes, a lecture in Indian-accented chemistry. Afterwards, his friends gather round him. Their eyes laugh and dance. They make very bad attempts at imitating this substitute accent. Then Bruce, one of his closest friends, turns to him and says, "Ashok, too bad he wasn't our regular teacher." Why? "Cuz then you could have gone"—and he gestures high-five-ish like we've seen the basketball and black sitcom stars do on TV—"hey, bloood, wha's up?" And Bruce laughs. Friends laugh. Ashok, an unlikely substitute, laughs.

What seems important here about Bruce's response to the substitute is the way the presence of another brown body accentuates and refines the way the brown student is perceived. However, within a white environment where race is rarely recognized on a conscious in-our-midst form, racialization is seen as any form of articulated "nonwhiteness." In this case, Bruce manifests this by suggesting there *should* be some sort of racial bond between the brown substitute and the brown student, but most outrageously suggests that the language accompanying this bond would be a type of learned-from-television Ebonics. That is, after all, how white culture learns about racialized people when they live in largely white communities: through the media images that are largely controlled and operated by white corporate interests! The brown student *becomes* the substitute in that student and teacher are racialized as one individual, and, going much further, the brown student substitutes for, becomes the embodiment of, racialized people within the white imaginary. In this case, the white imaginary narrowly conceives of racialized people not just as black but specifically as African American. If the so-called white-man's burden is dealing with the histories of slavery and the subjugation of peoples of color, then perhaps this particular brown student's burden is to represent all peoples of color *for* the benefit of his white colleagues.

WORDS THAT WOUND

This white imaginary, though, does possess the ability to differentiate racialized groups when it deems it necessary. Typical examples of this include the white imaginary's desire to find (and name) the *good* people of color who can stand out against the backdrop of apparently *bad* people of color. Multicultural agents often suggest, for instance, that immigrants from certain countries are "model citizens" as they learn to adapt to nationalist customs and laws. Such differentiation does little to combat the real problem of white supremacy, which posits itself as a standard by which others are measured (and by which *most* others fare badly). Internalized racism most often materializes as a result, with certain communities of color trying to distance themselves from other communities of color in order to benefit from white-supremacist institutions; on an individual level, this means people of color will frequently try to pass for white, and if that is not possible physically, then other methods of becoming white are favored, not the least of which is the adoption of racist values and judgements. But another, and more recognized, side to the internalized-racism argument is that, once interpellated as a racially inferior being, the person of color comes to loathe himself or herself and his or her racial community. In the following and last story about substitutions, the brown student and a white student are both similarly hazed as a frosh initiation process. The rite itself is fairly innocuous and certainly nonviolent, at least in terms of the physical gesturing. However, the accompanying racial epithets are far more damaging to the brown student. Keep in mind that, not unlike being interpellated by an unknown substitute teacher as a troublemaker, the student is here interpellated as a "paki," again by perpetrators to whom he is unknown except through his racial markings:

STORY THREE: Back up to the beginning of the same school year, grade ten, week two or three or whichever week they call frosh week (this occurring years before frosh "activities" are banned in many places). Walking across the overpass to Dr. E. P. Scarlett High School (named after a famous Calgary heart surgeon) and then down the hill, they can see the back entrance of the school, only a soccer field away. And as they approach (Ashok and his friend, Hank) they notice three students by the back entrance, sitting on the rail, hands sullenly behind backs. By the time they get to the asphalt circling the school moat-like, the three students, the "young toughs," move from their rail perch and lean toward the frosh students. Their eyes are liquid and excited. They have weapons, not the type you hear about in inner-city danger-zone schools, but the weapons of frosh week in suburbia: cans of shaving cream ha ha ha. They converge. Hank pulls away first; it takes Ashok a second more to break the grasp of the grade-eleven student who grabs his coat collar, shaving cream just barely foaming off the side of his head and down his shoulder. But when he breaks free, Hank just a few feet ahead of him and well within earshot, the grade-eleven student's voice rings clear: "Get him, get the paki, don't let the paki get away." Ashok is more covered in words—words that he has never *heard* before in association with himself—than in shaving cream. Hank and Ashok get past the entrance doors, into the safe haven of high school. Words are still sounding in his ears, but now they are from Hank, his friend Hank, Hank who thinks it's so funny that he keeps repeating the words. "Get the paki," he says. "Wasn't that funny? Get the paki. Get the paki. Get."

Once they have made it through the gauntlet, the brown student still hears the resonance of the racial epithets in his ears. But what resounds more is the reutterance of these demeaning remarks by his supposed friend; what is more damaging, perhaps, is the reiteration of these remarks *as if* they were humorous. To be called down by someone who hates you or mistrusts you is one thing; to be called down in the same way by a trusted friend is another. This particular form of naming—and the way this interpellation of the brown student is *shared* among white folks who do not know each other—brings the brown student into a place of raised awareness about the privilege of whiteness. If the brown student can see whiteness operate at levels that are intimate (by his friend) as well as hostile (by the hazers), the following connections can be made: (white) friends can easily be hostile in their intimacy *and* (white) strangers can be intimate in their hostility. That is, the power of whiteness allows Hank into the world of the white aggressors, in a way shifting their aggressive actions away from Hank, with whom *they* share a common bond: the aggressive actions toward a nonwhite, a paki. But also, and in some ways more insidious, the white strangers enforce an unwelcome intimacy by bestowing upon the brown student a name that insinuates a familiarity with *who* that brown student *is*. Put another way, the white strangers bestow upon themselves a degree of power and privilege by hailing the brown student in a way that puts them in an already familiar relationship with him that he does not have with them. Seen still another way, terms of racial derogation such as "paki," as used by the white folks (both friend and strangers), take on the familiar value of the French *tu*, albeit with a foregrounded component of contempt. In return, the brown student cannot reply with a similar familiar taunt, because calling the white interpellators "paki" would border on the ridiculous. And there is no term that carries with it a similar degree of the hostile and the familiar for white people *within* a white-supremacist regime. Thus, the brown student becomes resigned, in a way, to accept that familiar interpellation each and every time it is uttered for his benefit. The theoretical and practical question is, of course, how can we work ourselves out from under such a weighty system of oppression? Perhaps the answer lies in the analysis itself. If we can recognize the variety of systemic powers involved and how they operate to define and then confine our particular identities, then we can begin to liberate ourselves—through individual and collective, artistic, and academic action.

A WORD AFTER

As always when I come to the conclusion of a piece that attempts to deal with systemic oppression, I find myself asking whether this storytelling and analysis is actually promoting systemic change. Paulo Freire has said that for teaching to be a truly liberatory act, the components of reflection *and* action must be present interactively or the cause is likely lost. Here I wonder whether what I write resides too much on the reflective side, or if, perhaps, the action is indeed located in the writing and reading in the interstices of these stories. This is not to say that telling our stories is not a crucial element in dealing with racial abuse under a white-supremacist regime; rather, the question that poses itself is: after the story, then what? In a rather optimistic mode I would suggest that the telling of these stories can be a radical act if we resist opposition and keep telling them, repeating them to people inside *and* outside our various communities, and insist on being heard and addressed by the powers that be. It is, after all, this insistence on storytelling that confronted the Canadian government and forced it to redress Japanese Canadians who were wrongfully evacuated from the west coast and interred during the Second World War. And this refusal to submit, this hardy reliance on storytelling from the Gitksan We'tsuwet'in Nation is what brought the Supreme Court to its somewhat tardy recognition that the government needed to address land claims that will ultimately influence other First Nations claims in Canada. And while these might be seen as success stories of Pyrrhic proportions—that is, getting governments to admit past wrongdoings and create compensation packages for acts that should not have occurred in the first place—perhaps this is a beginning to a more positive spin to the act of storytelling. I would like to end on that note, but my pessimism overtakes me and I have to say that for all the potentially positive action that such storytelling catalyzes, there are countless stories that remain unheard, or if heard, certainly unlistened to, unacted upon, and buried alongside other acts of hate.

WORKS CITED

Althusser, Louis. "Ideology and Ideological State Apparatuses (Notes Toward an Investigation)." In *Lenin and Philosophy and Other Essays.* Trans. Ben Brewster. London: New Left Books, 1971: 121–73.

Bhaggiyadatta, Krisantha Sri. *Aay, Wha' Kinda Indian Arr U?* Toronto: Up Press (Un)Ltd., 1997.

Butler, Judith. *Excitable Speech: A Politics of the Performative.* New York: Routledge, 1997.

Freire, Paulo. *Pedagogy of the Oppressed.* Trans. Myra Bergman Ramos. New York: Continuum, 1993.

Matsuda, Mari, Richard Delgado, and Charles R. Lawrence, eds. *Words That Wound: Critical Race Theory, Assaultive Speech, and the First Amendment (New Perspectives on Law, Culture, and Society).* Boulder: Westview, 1993.

Mootoo, Shani. *Cereus Blooms at Night.* Vancouver, B.C.: Press Gang, 1996.

6

✿

Fire at My Face:
Growing Up Immigrant

Ritz Chow

IMMIGRANT MARKETS: THE COST OF CULTURE

In the crowds in Chinatown, along the streets where women and men huddle with cartons of colorful vegetables and take my dollar with gloved hands revealing their dark, soiled fingers, I am anonymous. Only here may I blend into the human throng, move into the flow of Asian faces. It is here where I feel most a stranger, my face admitting something my mind, clothes, and mannerisms do not. When I open my mouth to engage in conversation with store clerks and waiters, my alienation is complete. Language reveals me. My clumsy mouth falters on what few Cantonese words I know. Language demarcates the places of my "not-belonging" as much as my flat nose, my wide cheeks. Chinatown haunts me with its reminder that I do not belong.

Over the past twenty years, many Asian Canadians and Asian Americans have written about growing up in Chinatown. Yet how many have remained in the Chinatown houses of their parents and grandparents? Is there a legacy of moving out of Chinatown? Emigrating from Hong Kong to Canada as a child, I can, as the saying goes, take myself out of Chinatown but I can't take Chinatown out of me. However, for my parents, who emigrated to Canada as adults, Chinatown is a site where they may buy and eat familiar foods, where they are literate and in

105

the euphemistic know, where they can speak and be heard, and where my father has worked since our arrival in Canada. As much as they are literate there, I am illiterate. My tongue trips and I point and fumble with menus.

I pause at the juncture of voice and silence. Both silence and voice allow me entrances into belonging as surely as they delineate my exile. In the Canadian structure of multiculturalism, my cultural heritage resides on my body when I am silent. I am the one with whom non-Asian strangers, mostly White-looking, speak knowingly about sweet-and-sour chicken balls and egg rolls. In my silence, what multiculturalism has introduced is a means by which some, presumably "established Canadians," may access the cultures of "new Canadians" through the physical and psychical palate.

When I walk through Toronto's main Chinatown, which stretches along Dundas Street and Spadina Avenue, no one knows I fumble with Cantonese yet am fluent in English. Beside me, two White men with cameras around their necks stop to gawk at a magazine hanging in a bookstore window. They guffaw. Look at that, they drawl, they even have a Chinese *Playboy*! We have to get one, they declare to their White wives. I could be another curio along with the porcelain teacups, the chopsticks and incense—if only I do not open my mouth.

Canadian social activists and scholars such as Himani Bannerji offer critiques of the ongoing marketing and fetishizing of ethnicity. Different peoples and their cultures are reduced to objects that signify their foreign or exotic shades: edible objects such as dim sum, curry, and roti; cultural practices such as yoga and Buddhism, which are taken out of context, out of time and place. In addition, culturally sexist stereotypes of Asian women as sexually kinky, submissive sex workers, and mail-order brides, and as nimble-fingered and manually dexterous factory workers dominate the labor landscape in the global economic market. Much of the global and international economies rely on the exploitation of the bodies of young Asian women and the simultaneous fortification of their cultural stereotypes. Yet would the ethnic economic market work if the workers and products were to talk back? Talk back in effortless, "accentless" or properly accented English? What if fortune cookies contained slips of updated versions of diasporic Asian philosophical thinking?

Crack open an after-dinner cookie and find: "Your racist ways will choke you as surely as the food we serve is exotic." Ah, make it so.

The international ethnic markets present a plethora of racist, sexist, and heterosexist interpretations of what it means to embody a particular gendered cultural identity. To effectively challenge and resist cultural stereotypes and exploitation within North America, we must envision resistant acts that address both local and global capitalist ventures and market economies, and that carefully consider long-term benefits in lieu of short-term gains. We must challenge the ways in which aspects of capitalism threaten to dehumanize all of us. We must be critical of societal leniency toward people who perpetuate and advocate violence against people based on grounds of culture, gender, sexual identity, physical and psychological disabilities, and class. In order to mount an effective resistance, we need to know who we are as Asian Canadians and Asian Americans in history.

TOO CANADIAN AND NOT ENOUGH

I am a Chinese artifact. Two boys on the street call out "Chink," make nasal sounds and incoherent noises as I walk my seven-year-old body along First Avenue, which branches out of Toronto's East Chinatown toward my house by the railroad tracks at the end of a dead-end street. They watch me approaching, have something between them, jostle one another in the bid to deliver the quick flash of a Bic lighter at my face. They snarl past. Directed heat and smell of butane. Fire at my face. I pass flinching a little but never showing too much—masking the fear of fire, mouth closed and lips set. On the streets, I watch my parents being pushed by White teenagers who make sounds in a falsetto in their attempt to deride what they do not know. Cantonese? Mandarin? Toisan? While walking home, White boys and girls I do not know try out their bigger bodies and voices on me.

Last summer, I froze on the sidewalk on hearing similar sounds projected my way. Fear and rage and I turned to a two-feet-high girl with curly brown locks eyeing me from her yard. Something about the afternoon light, something about freezing in the summer of that noise, that ancient sound which burns like a fire at my face.

Growing up with my Chinese parents in Toronto, I am "too Canadian" for my parents, which is another way of saying I am not "Chinese enough." Yet are my parents' cultural notions of being Chinese dated and stagnant? Did their participation in Chinese culture end when we left Hong Kong over twenty-five years ago? If culture is inextricably bound to everyday realities and material existence, where and how is Chinese culture moving? Must diasporic Chinese people look to China and Hong Kong for cultural direction? Or are all diasporic cultures, in their bid for physical survival, forced to move quickly and irrevocably toward money?

When I was younger, the state's organization of labor was overtly related to immigration policies: my social-insurance card was issued by the Department of Employment and Immigration. Although government departments have changed, immigrants—especially immigrants of color—are still permitted entry into Canada according to their labor potential. In the current federal Live-In Caregiver program, Filipino women are issued work visas that specify their labor location and restrict their labor potential, thereby reducing these women to geographical origins: where they're originally from is what they do.

In the early 1970s, my parents and I entered Canada on the basis of immigrant labor needs. Luck, not chance, heralded our arrival. My father worked in the restaurant business and my mother entered a factory—historically appropriate jobs for Asians at the time. My parents and relatives in the United States and Canada stressed to my cousins and me at a young age the importance of an education. With an education, we would have more opportunities to get good jobs—perhaps better jobs than what first-generation Asian Canadians and Asian Americans such as my parents and their siblings could find. Yet, more than wanting their children to do well, I believe first-generation Asian Canadians and Asian Americans know too well the limitations that migration has imposed on their labor and life opportunities. To become a Canadian, then, is to unyoke one's labor potential from one's geographical origin and cultural background. Education was perceived as the great equalizer. Education would increase and expand one's labor potential and position. If we are what we do, then an education would enable us to be who we

Figure 1. Vincent Chin's mother with a picture of her son, July 14, 1983. Vincent was killed by unemployed auto workers in Detroit because they thought he was Japanese. Credit: Oakland Tribune/ Photo by Lonnie Wilson. Reprinted with permission from Oakland Tribune.

Figure 2. Boy in mourning clothes at the funeral of Ming Hai "Jim" Loo, who was attacked and killed in 1989 in Raleigh, North Carolina, because the perpetrators thought he was Vietnamese. Credit: Raleigh News and Observer/Photo by Gary Allen. Reprinted with permission from the North Carolina State Archives and North Carolina Department of Cultural Resources.

Figure 3. Norman Fong and Anna Chang at a rally in San Francisco on August 16, 1997, in remembrance of Kuan Chung Kao, slain by police in his Sonoma County, California, home. Reprinted with permission from the Asian Law Caucus (photographer unknown).

Figure 4. Christmas dinner at the Scott Mission in Toronto. Edmond Wai Hong Yu is enjoying his turkey dinner and chanting prayers over a lit candle. Edmond Yu, a homeless man, was killed on February 20, 1997, by Toronto police when he threatened them with a toy hammer. Credit: Toronto Star/Photo by D. Loek. Reprinted with permission from Toronto Star.

Figure 5. Eric Mar, marching in May 1996 at a rally against Proposition 209, coordinated with the National Organization for Women and the Rainbow Coalition. Photo by David Bacon and Scott Braley. Reprinted with permission from the Asian Law Caucus.

Figure 6. At a press conference addressing anti-Asian violence, Angelo Ancheta releases the results of the 1995 National Audit on Anti-Asian Violence. Reprinted with permission from the Asian Law Caucus (photographer unknown).

Figure 7. Ismael Ileto, brother of hate-crime victim Joseph Santos Ileto, speaks out against hate crimes at a 1999 rally in Los Angeles. Joseph Santos Ileto was a post-office employee shot by Buford Furrow, a white supremacist. Credit: Photo by Jamie Watson. Reprinted with permission from the APALC (Asian Pacific American Legal Center).

Figure 8. Southern California, 1996: The campaign poster of a Korean American candidate, sprayed with a swastika graffito. Credit: 1996 NAPALC audit (photographer unknown). Reprinted with permission from the APALC.

Figure 9. A unity march: elected officials, alongside the Reverend Jesse Jackson, march against hate in 1999. Photo by Jamie Watson. Reprinted with permission from the APALC.

Figure 10. APALC and a multicultural collaborative pull together a diverse alliance to speak out against hate crimes in Los Angeles, 1999. Photo by Jamie Watson. Reprinted with permission from the APALC.

Figure 11. Residents of San Francisco's Sunset District march against hate in 1999. Credit: Chinese World Journal/Photo by Portia Li.

Figure 12. An anti-Asian graffito in Palisades Park, New Jersey, October 1999. Photo by Dee Portera and Charles Portera II. Reprinted with permission of the Bergen Newspaper Group.

WHAT ABOUT US WHITE'S

We are being so screwed! We are being DEIGNED of a every opportunity that is giving to THE CHINESE. Look around, do you rent from a Chinese, do you buy your food from one? Do you buy your gas from one, or how about going to a fast food place, see any white people behind the counter? Walk down any street and count the china man. We are out numbered.

WAKE UP

Do you really think they give a shit about us. Go to China and try and buy land. White's can't own anything there. We are being ripped off by these sneaky little yellow fuckers and we can't do a damn thing about it. They come into our neighborhoods, buy our property, rip out anything that grows, mostly the trees, tear down our homes, and build ugly boxes for more Chinese. Count how many live on your block. Count how many own the houses on your block. Count how many who don't even speak our language. THIS HAS GOT TO STOP. STOP BUYING FROM THEM, STOP SELLING TO THEM, DEMAND THAT THE SPEAK ENGLISH, DEMAND THAT THEY STOP STEALING FROM YOUR TRASH, DEMAND THAT THEY EITHER GET A GREEN CARD OR GO BACK FROM WHERE EVER THEY CRAWLED OUT OF. DO YOU REALLY THINK THY GIVE A SHIT ABOUT US AMERICANS. I CAN TELL YOU, THEY DON'T. ALL THEY WANT IS WHAT WE HAVE. AND THEY WILL DO ANYTHING TO GET IT.

STOP THE YELLOW SCUM

DO SOMETHING TODAY FOR US WHITE PEOPLE, GET THEM WHERE IT HURTS. RIP THEM OFF. SPIT ON THEM, FLIP THEM OFF, ANYTHING, BUT DO SOMETHING. THINK ABOUT IT. PUT YOUR BOOT WHERE IT COUNTS.

GET THEM FIRST AND GET THEM GOOD! THEY WILL DO IT TO YOU!

Figure 13. The hate flyers shown in figures 13 and 14 were among those distributed to merchants in San Francisco's Outer Sunset neighborhood in 1999.

Figure 14. See figure 13.

Figure 15. Suman Virk with a photo of her daughters as small children. Her daughter Reena Virk (on the left) was beaten and drowned at age fourteen by seventeen-year-old Kelly Ellard and several other teens in Victoria, Canada, on November 3, 1998. Credit: Vancouver Sun/Photo by Peter Blashill. Reprinted with permission from the Vancouver Sun.

Figure 16. An anti-hate demonstration in Surrey, Canada, for the deceased Nirmal Singh Gill, who was killed by skinheads on May 6, 1998. The leader of the Sikh temple is thanking marchers for their support. Credit: Vancouver Sun/Photo by David Clark. Reprinted with permission from the Vancouver Sun.

want to be. "Freedom to labor" translates to "freedom to be." Further, if what we do is valued, we as a people become more valuable. We yearn to become integral to the country in which we work and live.

When I graduated from the University of Toronto, I crossed boundaries of social class and culture. I saw my parents trapped in the quagmire of old, traditional Chinese views. I strove to move away from the kind of Asian immigrants I perceived them to be: unfamiliar with the English language and, as such, easy targets for racial harassment and discrimination. The educational attainment and financial stability my parents had wished for me served to separate us culturally and psychically. Rather than separate us, did my parents think a Canadian education would allow my brother and me to become versions of themselves—albeit with better jobs?

The generational gap for immigrants, especially working-class immigrants, has an added, interwoven conflict connected to a contest of cultures in relation to capitalism. Academic and political theorists Roxana Ng and Chandra Talpade Mohanty have separately noted that the forces of capitalism—in Canada and the United States, respectively—position immigrants not only as cheap labor but also as inauthentic citizens. Immigrants serve to provide the physical, not intellectual, labor of a country or nation. As such, their expected participation as citizens resides mainly on what their bodies may do or, more accurately, endure—not what their ideas may contribute toward the governance and cultural growth of their new countries. While my parents arrived in Canada as working-class immigrants, my university education permits me to rebound off the construct of "working-class" and, in that very gesture, to destabilize the notion of "immigrant." Via my Canadian educational acculturation, I arrive as a Canadian citizen who lays claim to a country that she knows and whose citizens she expects to know of her.

What many children of Asian immigrants have become is another kind of Asian—an unrecognizable version of our parents' children. However, my search for Canadian belonging necessitated an estrangement from the only ancestral home I knew: my parents. Some of us realize our estrangement and try to reconnect with our roots. We note our tenuous Canadian identity—witness our Asian bodies falling prey to intense scrutiny and suspicion in times of economic crises, in debates of nationalism and boundaries. We inhabit the space of the never-ending exile. To understand this location, we talk with our parents and elders if they are still alive. We fly across oceans to land in a crowded and rushed Hong Kong or Tokyo, to sit in an old bus bouncing on dusty roads toward a remote part of China, or Indonesia, or Vietnam. We assemble and reassemble with placards and warm coats, shout out slogans as we walk, lean hard into days of "go home, Chink!," move shakily from unseen hands pushing us off buses, along subway platforms. Me, I try to bridge the distance with words, with black-and-blue smudges on a flat, white page—a woman smoothing her heritage with the heel of a palm and a scratch of ink. It's the only way I can keep myself from hating back.

CHANGED EXPECTATIONS

After completing two undergraduate degrees and working through a graduate degree, I am wary of the simplistic assumption that an education equals a good job equals a valued citizen. Even as immigrants move into jobs usually reserved for "unquestioned Canadians"—that is, those whose Canadian citizenship is rarely challenged in the streets or in impersonal public encounters—we retain the currency of "newness," of inauthenticity. In the pharmacy, I can don my white lab coat, do the health-professional routine, and feel valued for the advice I offer until the next racist, sexist, or heterosexist comment tries my workday. On the streets, I am just an Asian woman in a cotton jacket and blue jeans. On the streets, I get jostled, snarled at, pushed off buses, like any other Asian woman finding herself at the wrong place, beside the wrong White woman, or wrong man of any sort, at the wrong time.

With a Canadian education, what is not expected is that expectations change. What immigrants want and need change with every generation, with everyday practices that involve us in Canada and the very basics of living. Certainly, I am what I do in the labor market and I have opportunities that my parents' generation never did, but I now find myself pulled in different directions. I've followed the "good children of Asian immigrants" assimilation script: attend university, work in a professional field, make friends with diverse (non-Asian) folks, and pay taxes. Yet why do I see myself in my mother's shoes? Why am I called back to my childhood where I witnessed White teenagers accost my mother? Been there, done that. I thought that I would outgrow bullying and racist taunts, thought I'd left it all back in my childhood. Like Frantz Fanon before me, I now inhabit a place of anger. Or, as bell hooks writes, a place of "killing rage." What's a good immigrant to do when she turns away from her prescribed script? Education opens unexpected and dangerous doors. As hooks proposes, educators should "teach to transgress." This is the lesson I want to learn. Tell me how to transgress.

TOOLS FOR TRANSGRESSION

Reacting to and acting against racial violence is an intensely visceral and exhausting struggle for peoples of color whose bodies are all-too-visible targets for hatred. As an Asian Canadian girl and now woman, I used to wish that I were a big, strong Black woman. If I were big and Black, I thought, no White folks would dare to harass me or push me around. But after reading writings by African Americans and African Canadians, I realize that such an image is part of the history of Black stereotypes. The perceived strength of Blackness often translates to a hostile fear of Black folks. Racist policing, lynching, and the rape of Black women are examples of the structural hostility with which Black folks are met. As an Asian Canadian woman, I have not escaped the ethnic slurs that my parents used against people of other cultures. I was brought up to fear White and Black folks—in fact, anyone who was not Chinese. My parents' attitudes are all too commonplace in this society where we are taught to fear difference and to uncritically seek and find solace in sameness.

In writing about differences in the lives of women in American society, Audre Lorde notes that "crucibles of difference" separate women into categories of acceptability and unacceptability such that women are made wary and suspicious of differences, of each other. Lorde appeals to feminists to not allow notions of difference to separate them as they work against oppression. She

problematizes the concept of difference by noting that its patri-
archal function is separation. Rather than disposing of "difference," Lorde advocates revaluing its place in our lives. She
writes, "Difference must be not merely tolerated, but seen as a
fund of necessary polarities between which our creativity can
spark like a dialectic."

Since the publication of Lorde's essay, the integral and contradictory role of "difference" in political solidarity has sparked the
imagination of theorists and political activists. Perhaps Lorde's
"crucibles of difference" also serve to separate immigrants into
categories of acceptability and unacceptability. Also, do "crucibles of difference" separate Asians in a similar fashion? Yet, in
order to assert our unique cultural traditions and heritage, we
must emphasize our differences from other cultures. The issue is
not that we are different, but that "difference" is used to divide
us. The trick is to realize that strategies and their frameworks
and nuances can be used to our advantage and detriment. For
example, do we use the same or similar tools for our struggles
for freedom as have been used against us? Eye for an eye? Or do
we use "opposite" strategies? In place of hate, do we advocate
love? In place of violence, do we promote peace? As a departure
from loud protests, AIDS activists opted for the silence of "die-
ins," where they would lie down on sidewalks and roads while
their bodies were outlined with chalk. Is it a matter of using
whatever we've got? And exactly what have we got? Personal
ethics? Moral decency? Humanity?

The appeal to abstract notions—such as "humanity" and "personhood"—that seem to reach positively across differences is
common. Rod Michalko notes that a "persons-first" language exists in the disability-rights movement and in all human-rights
movements. "Persons-first" language presents the argument of
sameness in the name of personhood—that is, we are all persons
and therefore we are all entitled to the same rights. The problem
with a "persons-first" approach for disability culture, Michalko
argues, is that it obliterates the identities of people with disabilities by avoiding and subsuming differences. Simultaneously, a
"persons-first" approach creates a situation whereby people
with disabilities are pressured to show just how nondisabled
they are—just how well they fit into the Western notion of personhood—in order to lay claim to rights.

To me as an Asian immigrant, Michalko's argument strikes close to home. In my struggles to be acknowledged as a Canadian citizen, I often must emphasize how well I fit into mainstream Canadian society by downplaying my "Asianness." Although differences among Asian people are often denied in order to maintain a sense of cultural coherence, ironically, most of us would not hesitate to announce how we differ from other Asians when we want to emphasize our Canadian credentials. One truly becomes a Canadian when one can participate in xenophobic and anti-immigrant comments. To belong, it seems, involves renouncing differences.

As peoples of color, we must be wary of political positions and structures that set us up to jostle and fight each other for a foothold. As diasporic Asians, we must consider the differences within our cultures—in terms of gender, class, physical and psychological disabilities, and sexual identity. If one is already different, why stand out more? Would anyone say a Canadian is an Asian feminist who identifies as a lesbian? What is your mental picture of a Canadian? For many Asian Canadians, we are our own image of Canadian.

Audre Lorde's critical examination of difference points to important strategies for Asian Canadians and Asian Americans as they struggle against racist violence. First, we must not allow our differences to be used against us. In addition, we must reevaluate the various and, at times, contradictory strategies employed in our antioppressive struggles. Second, we must consider and reconsider what tools and strategies are necessary to address racial hatred. Finally, we must find a place to work out our anger, to constructively let loose our rage. We must acknowledge the desire for revenge and the temptations to hate back.

CRITICAL SILENCES

Much of my childhood and adulthood has been spent in silence when confronted with anti-Asian violence, whether physical or vocal. As a feminist, I have learned the value of "breaking silences" and the importance of "voice" in antioppressive struggles. Yet, I am reluctant to view the act of "speaking out" or "giving voice" as the solution to addressing antiracist violence. If that were the solution, my throat would become hoarse with re-sistance.

As a young child, I learned the complexities of silence. I was designated the loud one by my mother because I talked and let the family secrets out. Words issuing from my mouth would be-tray me. Yet I could not recall what I'd said, what my words had transgressed. For protection, I resorted to silence. My silence was so pure nothing could infiltrate what I wouldn't say. The more I didn't say, the less my mother knew. Silence denied knowledge and circumvented blame. In not saying, I would never have to unsay. Assuming a stance of silence located me as a "strange child," one whom relatives considered "too mature" for my age. Yet they would search for a positive identification, labeling me as *"see-mun"* or ladylike: quiet and obedient. My mother and I knew the label was a misnomer. My silence was about not being *"see-mun,"* it was about rebellion. I countered my mother's bar-rage of words with a wall of silence. If words were her weapon, silence was my amulet.

My mother's silence, however, was a different entity. My mother's silence was a horrible beast. It hovered and stalked the small spaces. It threatened to burst, to roar, and to strike. The longer the silence, the greater the beast, the more sustained would be her beating and final release of words and sound. She said I caused the buildup of her rage. She would say to me, *"nee gick do au say"* or "you pressure me to the point of death." I per-ceive the word *"gick"* as bound to the pressure of silence on the body; an internal rather than an external pressure. As if my mother boiled her silent rage, her body like the slow-cooker with the melted plastic legs atop our stove. In the struggles between my mother and me, silence had veritable shape and weight. What spaces does silence occupy?

Was my mother's rage related to her location as an immigrant woman in the 1970s' heyday of multiculturalist politics in Canada? Into which locations have Asian Canadians been in-serted via the selling of Canada as a multicultural nation in the 1970s? How has multiculturalism been utilized to mask the fed-eral government's move to divert attention from Québecois and aboriginal peoples? What is the price of immigration now and then? What does multiculturalism require of us?

When I think of multiculturalism, the image in my mind is that of a cluster of "happy immigrants" waving small Canadian flags. Something about generosity. Something about tolerance. To "them." To me. Feminist psychologists Nikki Gerrard and Nayyar Javed have noted that immigrants are expected to be grateful for what Canada offers them, especially what is not available to them in their home countries. Writer Austin Clarke notes, "Gratitude, one of the aspects of 'exile' in its most traditional sense, is exemplified by a silence of criticism of the country offering this 'exile.'"

COMING TO CRITICISM

On pense où on a les pieds[1] (a Québecois saying)

At times, silence is unbearable, the way words are ripe against the skin of the moment. Situations in my childhood have located me at different sides of silence. Silence has been imposed yet I have also chosen silence. I know the ambiguity of words and of silence; ours is an unstable relationship. I mistrust silence and words even as I rely on them.

When I "came out" into the Toronto lesbian feminist community in the late 1980s, speech was still at its prime. I came across Audre Lorde's quote, "My silences had not protected me. Your silence will not protect you." Bound to these two sentences is a sense of insurgency and rage that encapsulated the drive and push of second-wave feminism. Lorde stressed the importance of speaking out, especially as she reflected upon her diagnosis with cancer. She reflected that "death . . . is the final silence" and advocated the breaking of silences; however, she was not oblivious to the risks that speech entailed. There is a cost for speaking, especially if one is an outsider. Yet Lorde maintained that speaking out is worth the costs and the very real risks.

When I came out, I began to talk. I used the ragged words, the uneven platform of the page and put down my past. I spoke into the open silences of women, and their silences opened mine. Learning my place requires voice and silence. I read poetry and essays written by self-identified lesbians of color, survivors of various forms of abuse, disenchanted and disenfranchised peoples, fragile and strong women and men. Words converge and voices weave. I learn to name myself in text and in voice. The silence in my apartment comforts me; there I can think and read, think and listen. In the silence, I hear the beginning of myself.

During what is known as the second wave of the feminist movement, there was a proliferation of women's voices. Women were encouraged to speak from their locations of experience. Talk was peppered with phrases such as "the personal is political," "consciousness-raising," and "down with patriarchy." All these phrases are connected with the primacy of speech, of "breaking silence." Yet, how exactly do voices "break the silence"? Is there a manner of speaking, of writing that would more likely elicit an audience than not? In essence, "breaking silences" often translates into "being granted a hearing with one's oppressor." What is a voice when it is unheard? Although the importance of silence is now acknowledged, there still exists a hierarchy of voice over silence in feminist and nonfeminist realms. Voice is privileged, is contrasted and juxtaposed with silence in terms such as "speaking out" and "breaking silence." What is the relationship between silence and voice? Through a critical examination of voice and audience, feminists have reevaluated silence. The importance of what can't be said— "what the work cannot say" as Gayatri Spivak writes—has enriched feminist analyses.

Sociologist Sherene Razack notes that people of color are often asked to tell their stories to White audiences; they are commanded to enter dialogic spaces, to speak in prescribed manners. The forum of speech, of "breaking silence," is critical, then, in assessing the authoritative position and power of the speaker—and the listener. Gayatri Spivak speaks of "hegemonic people" who are "card-carrying listeners" in the intellectual spheres. In other words, Spivak argues that some folks occupy the powerful position of authenticating what is said by judging how it's said and the person who said it. The content and form of what is said and written, along with the location of the speaker or writer, determine who listens, who walks away. The emphasis on speaking out as the only form of resistance to racist violence and other forms of oppression is problematic since the act of "speaking out" may function as a red herring. You may say all you want to no avail. The preoccupation with saying it, with writing it down may obscure other methods of resistance, of challenging oppressive forces. What happened before women and other oppressed peoples "spoke out"? Were we just silent lambs to the slaughter? What about passive resistance? What about silent and subversive acts? Does silence become overshadowed by the primacy of voice? Has resistance become defined only within the parameters of voice? If we ignore other forms of resistance, do we victimize and alienate our potential allies in the struggle? Do we fall prey to Asian stereotypes by perceiving our silences to represent only passivity and weakness?

Psychologist Nayyar Javed suggests that silence is a vital part of the coping capacity and strategy of survivors of torture. In "A Dialogue about Racism and Silence," Javed writes that within the religious beliefs of Sufism, silence is perceived as a means by which energy is retained for survival. Further, silence offers and opens up space for inner dialogue. Part of the strategy, then, is silence; the other part, voice. By considering the many different strategies used to resist racist violence, we can learn to be flexible in our survival. We don't always need to be speaking out and fighting back against racist violence. We must also conserve energy to create, to love, to think and reflect, and to survive. We must respect and encourage the particular ways in which we individually choose to live and resist. In the face of racist violence, silence is not nothing, just as speaking out is not everything.

POINT, NO POINT (VANCOUVER ISLAND, BRITISH COLUMBIA)

by Ritz Chow

The ocean roars its wanton song.
Here, the fire makes small yelps,
leaps and jumps toward blood-
hot cheeks blazing borders
in this pine cabin we call retreat:
a rest from our every day
struggle with words.

Silence curls like your small dog
licking his inflamed skin,
cool tongue hanging with humidity.
Outside the rain pelts and patters,
soaks our lives with salt and seriousness
as we flicker adrift in shadows,
in years we have pushed past
to arrive at the shores of this night,
the Chinese in us steaming,
smoking evanescent trails,
taking this forest by storm.
Our wide cheeks and eyes tip
the green B.C. interior to a slant.
In our waterproof jackets,
made in Canada boots,
we haul extra sweaters over shoulders:
lives slung low tight against skin;
these packs we load with memories,
wet firewood, miles and miles of rain.

NOTE

1. Translation: One thinks where one has feet.

BIBLIOGRAPHY

Bannerji, Himani. 1995. *Thinking Through: Essays on Feminism, Marxism, and Anti-Racism*. Toronto: Women's Press.

Clarke, Austin. 1994. "Exile." In *Altogether Elsewhere: Writers on Exile*. Ed. Marc Robinson. San Diego: Harcourt Brace. 59–63.

Fanon, Frantz. 1967. *Black Skin, White Masks*. Trans. Charles Lam Markmann. New York: Grove Press.

Gerrard, Nikki, and Nayyar Javed. 1994. "A Dialogue about Racism and Silence: Personal and Political Perspectives." *Canadian Woman Studies* 14 (2): 64–67.

hooks, bell. 1995. *Killing Rage: Ending Racism*. New York: Henry Holt.

———. 1994. *Teaching to Transgress: Education as the Practice of Freedom*. New York: Routledge.

Lorde, Audre. 1984. *Sister Outsider: Essays and Speeches*. New York: Crossing Press.

Maclear, Kyo. 1994. "Not in So Many Words: Translating Silence across 'Difference.'" *Fireweed: A Feminist Quarterly of Writing, Politics, Art and Culture.* 44/45: 6–11.

Michalko, Rod. "Identity and the Language of Disability." Keynote speech, Paul Jones Memorial Symposium. The University of British Columbia, 10 March 2000.

Mohanty, Chandra Talpade. 1991. "Cartographies of Struggle: Third World Women and the Politics of Feminism." In *Third World Women and the Politics of Feminism.* Eds. Chandra Talpade Mohanty, Ann Russo, and Lourdes Torres. Bloomington: Indiana University Press. 1–47.

Ng, Roxana. 1993. "Sexism, Racism, Canadian Nationalism." In *Returning the Gaze: Essays on Racism, Feminism and Politics.* Ed. Himani Bannerji. Toronto: Sister Vision Press. 223–41.

Razack, Sherene. 1993. "Storytelling for Social Change." In *Returning the Gaze: Essays on Racism, Feminism and Politics.* Ed. Himani Bannerji. Toronto: Sister Vision Press. 100–122.

Spivak, Gayatri. 1988. "Can the Subaltern Speak?" In *Marxism and the Interpretation of Culture.* Eds. Cary Nelson and Lawrence Grossberg. Urbana: University of Illinois Press. 271–313.

III

GROWTH AND RESISTANCE

7

Am I Beautiful Now?

Jia Ling

In black and white, a piece of paper tacked to the entrance of my college dormitory read, "When a group of men were asked what they feared most about women, they replied, 'That they'll laugh at us.' When a group of women were asked what they feared most about men, they replied, 'That they'll kill us.' Your reality is not my reality."

I grew up watching shadows, listening for footsteps, and dodging whispers. I learned how to cross the street as if it had been my intention all along and not because of that one coming up from behind or you with your eyes on me. I became hypervigilant, a mouse living among cats, forever on guard.

This was my reality. At its extreme, fear inhabited me to the point where I might be crossing the street to get to my car, and all I could think about was what it would be like to have my throat slit, if I would feel the heat of my own blood, if there would be much pain, how long I would be able to see. I used to come out of my house, hiding my face from the street, because I didn't want any attention for anything from anyone who would know where to find me. And sometimes just knowing that someone was looking at me gave me the creeps. It could be a beautiful, sunny day, and all that would go through my mind was, It's that person right there, him by the tree, no, it will be that one over there, pacing back and forth, who will do it, who will follow me and kill me in my own home.

There are a thousand reasons to hate me, and you only need one person to do something about it.

Because I was a naturally shy little girl, it was almost to be expected that I found it beyond me to warm up to people, that I preferred to keep to myself. Quiet kids, by default, were unpopular. As it turned out, being one of the smarter kids in school didn't help either. But doing well in school was all I knew, and intellectualizing everything helped me take things in. I found several clubs to involve myself in, became an officer on the associated student-body board, ruled the school newspaper as editor in chief, and graduated at the top of my class. On paper, everything seemed perfect, but after the graduation ceremony, when my family members took turns embracing me, I remember thinking that it was the first time I had been held by anyone for years. Growing up without affection would eventually play its own destructive part.

Difficulty making friends, social ineptness, insecurity over looks. . . . Granted, trying to find your own beauty in a world composed of distorted mirrors is part of everyone's story, your basic coming-of-age pains. Though it doesn't make it right, certain rites and milestones seem universal enough. But how normal is it when kids you've never seen before call you a bitch and then threaten to beat you up if you look in their direction? To be backed against a chain-link fence and choked until you're not sure whether it's the grip on your throat or terror that has cut off your voice? To dread coming into contact with anyone new, for fear of being mimicked, taunted, or just silently sneered at? I cannot answer these questions; my perspective was thrown a long time ago. These were part of my reality before I even had a favorite color, before I was given my first teddy bear, before I knew that P came before Q. All I know is that I feel tampered with. I feel set up. I had to grow up on the defensive when I could have been looking forward to life.

I remember . . . how chilling it was just to hear the word *Chinese,* as if it were the N word, because I had almost never heard it said in a nonvicious context.

I remember . . . classmates mimicking Chinese speech as I walked by, trying their hardest to distort their faces so I would see how deformed I looked to them.

I remember . . . the physical invasion of my space and body—being slammed against the lockers, looking up at a sound and being hit in the head with trash, having my books knocked from my hands, being anonymously struck from behind.

Most of all, I remember the slurs. I have heard epithets shouted from cars, from across the street, from the hallway, from the seat behind me . . . even spoken casually by my teachers, my friends, my coworkers, my lovers. Often, I would only catch the tail end of it, the first part garbled in my subconscious. Or insults would be uttered under the breath and I would wake up at four in the morning with the words echoing in my head. It got so bad that sometimes I would hear something when there was no one around to say it.

When I relate such experiences, I am wary of blowing them out of proportion. Sometimes, I overcompensate by minimizing the impact, stepping gently over the details for fear of knocking over my own defenses. Partly, it is due to modesty—feeling guilty for indulging in old injuries and not wanting to bring attention to myself. On the other hand, I end up throwing out shocking lines without allowing them to have the weight they deserve—what I would expect from someone else.

So, in this personal piece, this is what I am trying to accomplish: for once, I want to give my stories of being hated the weight, the space, and the silence they deserve.

As a young child, I learned that I was ugly.

By the time I was ten, I had begun obsessing over what I didn't like about my appearance: thick glasses, crooked front teeth, androgynous body, straight dark hair, small eyes, and yellow skin. Somehow, I had traced these to being Asian, or, more accurately, the stereotype. To be Asian was to be ugly.

This is what I thought of myself for the first twenty years of my life. Ugliness is more than skin deep: if you believe yourself to be something, then you can become that. It was easy to manage, really, learning to see what others saw. I had nothing else to go on. So, at ten, I began the longest journey of my life: finding ways to be something other than myself.

As a child, I didn't know what to do. I felt hunted from all directions, but I was powerless to fight back. When I grew older, the answer became obvious: while I cannot single-handedly change society, I can always change myself. If I was still targeted, then it was clearly because I failed to change myself enough. It must have been. If it were this intangible entity called "society" at fault, that would completely take away any control I may have, and I would much rather blame myself, hate myself, change myself than stomach the thought of having zero control over what happened to me.

I wanted to fit in so badly I was willing to follow any script that was given to me. Part of this can be attributed to being an Asian female who is also a middle child; lucky me, I was thrice socialized to please, to want peace between everything and everyone. Things were quieter that way. Unfortunately, what my family wanted me to be and what I needed to be to fit in at school were contradictions. It wasn't even a matter of knowing what to pick and choose between the two institutions. If you mix black and white, you get neither; you get a muddy third color that no one asked for. At home, I was criticized for always sitting with my legs apart, walking like a boy, being too outspoken, and not liking babies. However, I also wasn't allowed to shave my legs, use deodorant, wear makeup, let my hair grow out long— all of which were like using soap and water for the other girls. The more my mother tried to control me, the more I sought to hide my "deviations" from her. I did not feel like I belonged any-where.

My mother's style of child-raising had been passed down from her mother before her: to get you to stop doing something, they just make you feel really awful about yourself until you change. It didn't register at the time, but this tactic completely mirrored the outside.

So I changed. I tried to alter my skin color by burning myself under the sun. Contacts replaced my glasses, which I'd had to wear since the first grade. I got braces and curled my hair. I went as far as consciously softening my voice and altering my body language, which were criticized as unfeminine. Until I was in my twenties, I couldn't even bear to look at myself in the mirror and speak English at the same time: those words coming out of that foreign face? Ugh.

So, caught between my family's version and society's version of how I should be, I tried to be both, alternately, depending on which world I was in. Model American student by day, good Chi-nese daughter by night. All the while, I repeated to myself, They can dictate your behavior, but they cannot dictate your thoughts; they can change your look, but they can't change you. I just prayed everyone would finally let me be. After a while, I began thinking of myself as two people, both false. And the only thing that the two parts created by this double bind had in common was that both my family and the "outside" still agreed that I was below standard: not girly enough, not White enough . . . ugly.

Meanwhile, going to school became a scheduled trauma. Day after week after month after year, I was forced by law to be around kids who went out of their way to remind me of my place in "their" world. When they pulled up the corners of their eyes like that, those were my eyes they wanted me to see. When they spewed mumble-jumble in that odd singsong voice, that's my embarrassing speech they wanted me to hear. For fun, they did this. And the more I was mocked, made to listen and look at their impressions of "Orientals," or had things thrown, yelled, or spat at me, the more I wanted to just . . . leave. Nothing I did, nothing I was, was pretty enough. But there was nowhere to go, except deeper inside myself. I became really good at not feeling or showing a damn thing.

For a while, this was very healing, partly because I was alone and I could think. Rather than seeking to be the opposite of ugly, which didn't work, I decided that I was to be neither ugly nor beautiful. I wanted to be a nothing, in between here and there, not this label nor that label, and may the gods help those who dared refer to me by my body, such as calling me a woman. I am not my body! I am my mind, and my mind is not tied to gender, race, age, or size. I am my mind, and my mind can be everything and nothing. With this philosophy, I cradled myself and found living tolerable. This was the next step in a very calculated and deliberate separation from my body.

I cloaked myself in baggy clothing and let my hair cover my face. My plan was to eradicate or hide any gender, race, or sexuality "markers," anything that would give me away. My awareness of stereotypes influenced my new appearance, on top of my severe detachment from my physical self. I identified almost purely as an intellectual being. (Yes, it is another stereotype of Asians that they are smart, so I failed a few classes to prove to myself I wasn't even that.) The more I split my mental dimension from the physical, the more at peace I was. As an outsider, now one of my own creation, I felt powerful. But this was true only as long as I stayed away from people; they can always find a way to make you feel like shit.

Now that I saw my body as a tool and not as a valid part of me, life became a series of experiments, and this flesh and these nerves served as my laboratory. Binge drinking became a hilarious diversion, but I couldn't kill my rationality. (Even though it has always been my way out, trying to stop thinking became a theme for the next few years.) I deliberately got lost, just to see if I could find my way back, and I forced myself to walk through the park late at night, precisely because I was afraid of doing so. And I started to have sex, for the same reasons—because I was tired of being afraid of touch. This experiment turned out to be a mistake.

I didn't realize how heavily it would resonate, being touched after so many years of quiet. Touch shocked me. It sent this awful echo inside my body. I felt it in my heart, scraping, as if I were rudely awakened from a deep sleep. For years, no affection; suddenly, this sexual touch came at me like electricity, like fire, and the contrast numbed me. Being detached gave me more control over my partners, over my experiments, but as I moved from number two to number three, on to numbers eight and nine, I started to become undone.

Over time, my mind had begun to give way to a flood of violent nonsequitur images—soundless little vignettes, looped for my involuntary viewing pleasure. They usually appeared for no reason at all; I could just be working my way through a regular day. In one of them, I very slowly draw a sharp blade down from my forehead, across the tip of my nose, over my lips, down my chin, over and over, until the image tires itself. This particular "daydream" emerged when people began telling me they thought I was beautiful. Yeah, that's a good one, tell the ugly chick she looks hot so she'll have sex with you.

Not used to getting positive attention for how I looked, I let the little compliments worm their way inside me, to where my ten-year-old self was listening. I think this is when I started to become sad again. My younger self let old hopes surface; unfortunately, she was a bad judge of character and liked everyone too fast, too much. The image of cutting my own face up was a warning as well as a purification ritual. It took me a long time to stop placing people coming on to me in the same category as people coming after me. Honestly, there was little difference, though the intentions of people who found you attractive were often more impure than those of people who hated you outright.

All those years while I had been trying to hold myself together by tearing myself apart, the world had been quietly changing. My old high school now had a "minority majority" (mostly Latin and Asian Americans), when I had been one of the few. Asian Americans were also getting more varied acting roles, and fewer strangers tried to test their three or four words of Chinese on me. So, things had gotten better on the outside, but what the hell was I doing to myself? There was a disheartening gap between the lessening ignorance in society and my own ignorance of how differently people had come to see me. What, am I beautiful now? Is it safe now?

I was clueless about what to do with myself. I didn't want to grow old not knowing how my truths fit in with everyone else's. I was ready to take everything I had, turn it upside down, and expose the roots. I wanted to stop feeling confused, sorry, frustrated, and tainted. I wanted to be at peace with the past, with all the things that I am, and hold them close. I was twenty-five, and I decided to take my body back.

Almost overnight, I stopped feeding relationships that I felt were bad for my soul, because I was tired of having to put up with all the little abuses that came with them. Almost everyone around me was straight, White, male, financially well-off, and never took seriously the things that concerned me as a non-straight, non-White, nonrich nonmale. They couldn't. Nothing in their personal histories resembled my own, and they often made me feel like I was creating problems by having a different take on things. So I just neatly removed myself from their little white-and-white lives, and never looked back.

I knew what I had to do. I wanted to surround myself with people who might relate to me. I wanted to see what it was like to have Asian friends, for once. It's not that I think individuals who share a few biological features have this magical bond with each other, but I figured, since we happen to look alike in these specific ways, ways in which we have been habitually categorized, how can we not share some stories? When I became involved with the Asian American community and became a part of the incredible diversity I found there, I stopped thinking of Asians as ugly when I saw myself in their faces; instead, I began thinking of myself as being as beautiful as they are.

Like all people, I am many things. The labels are endless. Sometimes, it's easy to tell what it is about you to which people are responding; other times, there is little to go on. To interpret all assaults and threats against me as "anti-Asian," though being Asian is probably the most obvious thing about me, is to ignore all other possible factors in favor of simplifying hatred. Hatred is never simple.

Rodney King, who went down in LAPD history, is Black, and racism became the most talked-about motive for the brutal beating that was immortalized on videotape. No one, however, seemed to acknowledge how the other parts of him played a part. He wasn't just Black, he was also a man, a young Black man of a certain class, as well as other things. All these elements had their own role in the severity, duration, and type of beating he received—even the very fact that it ever happened. Had any of those variables been different, Rodney King might have received a different response from the police officers. If he had been a she—but with the same body type, clothing, and behavior— would she have been beaten as severely or at all? I don't remember anyone crying sexism. Would the outcome have been the same if he were an old man or if he were dressed as a person of wealth—all other factors being equal? I don't remember anyone crying ageism or classism. Imagine if it had been a rich, elderly White woman who had led them on the chase. What happened did so because of everything they saw in him, a combination of labels, not race alone. His case is a paradigmatic example of how dislike of a part became dislike of the whole. In other words, if it's "normal" to be a White, middle-class, straight, adult male of medium build, and if I'm all of the above except I'm not White, forget it. In a bigot's eyes, that one exception negates the other "acceptable" features. It's another version of the one-drop theory used to categorize Blacks.

So, what am I? What do people see? What reasons have been given for people hating me?

I am the second daughter of poor immigrants from China. I went from the city of New York, my birthplace, to the city of

Los Angeles at the age of four. I am a classic peace-loving, riot-inciting middle child with one eyebrow permanently arched. I identify as an omnisexual, pansensual, gender-transcendental, androgyny-loving butch femme. I am on the side of human rights and animal rights, a lacto-ovo-vegetarian for over a decade, a feminist since birth. I am a nonmonogamous, non-promiscuous single person who completes herself. I have danced on the sidewalks of San Francisco, smoked pot by the L.A. River, and stood under paintings of myself in a Beverly Hills art gallery. I am a control queen by profession, a pathological truth-teller by nature, and a social chameleon by default. I am a thousand things and cannot and will not assume why certain people have certain reactions to me.

The cause-and-effect connection between feelings and behavior, by nature, is not something you can dissect and piece together in this fashion—especially not someone else's. Maybe if my test scores hadn't been so high, the other kids would not have waited to pick me to play on their teams. Maybe if I followed the latest clothing trends, I would have had more friends. Maybe if I wore lipstick, no one would treat me as if I were too young to be taken seriously.

My point is, the reasons are irrelevant—no one could possibly control everything about themselves, nor should they feel that they need to in order to survive. What does matter is that I stopped blaming myself. It is vital to our livelihood and to our future as a community that we embrace our differences buried underneath all this noise. This philosophy is the basis of my lifestyle now, but I had to cross my share of broken roads to get to this point.

I want to address a particular sentiment that I come across often, in the "good guys" camp, no less. Some people believe that people like me ought to step aside and let the "real" victims speak. That set next to "real" concerns—from war, to genocide, to slavery, to rape—my experiences are not worthy because they are not newsworthy. That if I have never been beaten up, mugged, raped, strung up on a tree limb, or nearly gassed in a chamber, then I have nothing else to add. This is how I feel about that:

Don't let anyone get off on quantifying your pain, counting the ways in which you have been shut out/shut off so they can be compared with other people's abuses. Don't let them tell you it's not your turn to speak, that there are more important stories out there, or we've heard all this before, so take a number. Don't think that being repeatedly pushed, taunted, cornered, laughed at, humiliated, spat on, and followed—for amusement—did not convulse every ounce of my being just because there was technically no crime committed. Don't let anyone make you feel ashamed for having been slapped.

I'm thirty now. Everything seems so long ago. My only recurring daydream is of tightly embracing someone, not of slicing my own face up. I don't think my fifteen-year-old brother has any idea what it's like to be attacked, racially or otherwise. The most popular kids at his school are Asian American. The arts, fashion, languages, and products of Asian cultures are now taking their turn being the "in" thing. While I see this as objectification, I do think it's about time I see more Asian faces in magazines and on television.

Even though I no longer fear my immediate surroundings, residual sadness still reveals itself parenthetically, like an afterthought. There will always be someone who thinks I'm not Asian enough, butch enough, old enough, or rich enough, but I can't be bothered by that anymore. We all need to find our balance, unwrap our essence, and, for yours truly, this means having fun being everything and nothing, this color and that color, ugly and beautiful. This is what it means for me to be whole.

8

❀

Newly Immigrated to America: A Narrative of Violence

Misa Kawai Joo

She seemed to smile at me from the front page of the newspaper, pink cheeked, black haired, dressed in a red jumper. The Laotian second grader should have been posing as a winner of a poetry contest or a spelling bee. Instead the story screamed of rape and murder.

The paper reported that the seven-year-old girl had not been in her classes that day. Both parents worked, the mother a stockroom clerk at a local department store and the father a cook at a restaurant. The school's attendance clerk failed to call either of them at work to check out their daughter's absence.

The mother arrived home to be with the children. Her daughter was alarmingly late when she finally called her husband to hurry home. I imagined them, frantic, as they packed up their young son and ran to the school, banging on the locked doors. The janitor had not seen their daughter. They called the teacher from the school phone, bold with fear. She gave them the shocking news that their daughter had not been in school all day. I imagined their terror.

The paper continued that the father had walked his daughter to school later than usual that morning, past the 7-eleven where students later reported to police a weird teenage boy who drove a white van and often stood watching them play. That particular day, the father walked her to the edge of the playground rather than taking his daughter into her classroom. He had to rush home to be with his young son, in bed with a stomachache. His last sight of his precious daughter was of her running happily toward the school door.

The paper recounted how her small body had been found dumped in a park by the Willamette River. A teenager in a white van had been apprehended and was in custody for the rape and murder. This was the same man the young children had witnessed loitering around the playground for days. Police found the back of the van littered with pornographic magazines.

My friend Peggy Nagae, a local attorney, and I felt moved to visit her family. We pushed away any thought that the family did not know us or that we may be interfering. We knew how lonely it was to be Asian in this city, scattered, without community neighborhoods, and believed it was probably even more difficult for new immigrants. I cooked something to take for the family just as we would have done back at home.

As I prepared the casserole, I remembered how my sister and I learned as small children about the dangers that lay outside the family circle. One memory stood out in my mind. We two children waited in the car for our mother and grandmother to come out of the store. Grandpa walked back and forth along the sidewalk, keeping his eyes on us. My family never left us unattended.

I saw a tall White man with a hat approach my grandfather at the end of the walk. The stranger talked to my grandfather and took something out of his pocket. Grandpa turned away toward the car and the stranger returned something to his pocket, walking away.

On the way home, I pretended to take a nap beside my sleeping sister in the backseat of our old Buick. Grandpa, I remember, talked about the stranger offering him money to leave the girls. I did not understand anything except the gray, damp feeling of fear. I remember the adults' shocking conversation about what kind of people lived in a place like this. As new immigrants themselves, my grandparents witnessed the violent face racism turns toward Asian people. During World War II, they experienced how suddenly people became hateful, confusing their Japanese American neighbors with "the enemy." My grandparents carefully taught their children and their grandchildren that violence toward children was a harsh reality and to beware.

The casserole finished, Peggy and I prepared to leave to visit the family. We discussed that rape of children must be inconceivable to a Laotian family. Did these new immigrant families ever suspect they would need to teach their young daughter to beware of people who ask for help? Did they say, "Do not accept candy from anyone you do not know?" Did they know to teach their beautiful little daughter to run away, screaming, from smiling strangers?

Taking along the address printed by the paper, Peggy and I arrived at the home of the girl's parents. It was puzzling to us that the paper would print the address of the victims. This proved to be the first of many puzzling exceptions to the rule the new immigrant family was to suffer. We were welcomed at the door by a slight young man, black hair flopped over to one side. He looked drained, but his ready smile came quickly, like a habit. He invited us in, two Japanese American women whom he'd never met.

He gestured toward the couch. His wife, the mother, sat stiffly in the shadows. I explained we had read the paper. She welcomed us to sit with her, but her face remained expressionless and silent. Sitting beside her, I could feel her tension. She reached out and held both our hands. That was our first meeting, but I was to have three more visits, which taught me more than I wanted to know about the vulnerable status of immigrant people in the United States.

The next time, I visited the family alone. That day the mother poured out her story. Her only daughter was her bright and shining star. She recalled how her mother's heart almost burst with pride when her daughter came home from school and announced, "Mama, I'm going to be a nurse when I grow up!"

"From that moment," she said, "I decided that I would make sure she could be a nurse! I knew the only way was for me to have an operation." I was bewildered. She continued, "I should not have more children so she can go to school."

Her words settled like a cold stone between us. "I cannot have any more children, no more daughters," she said aloud to herself.

"Sometimes they can change that," I wanted to reassure her. "You can have another operation which might reverse that."

"I cannot have anymore children," she repeated. "They took it all out."

My shock showed, "They didn't tell you there were other ways? Did they tell you about birth control?" I hated to be the one to tell her after the damage was done that the doctors were supposed to inform her of all the options—another exception put upon this family.

"No, I was not told," she said simply. "My life is ruined." Her face pinched shut with the feeling of betrayal.

Just then, her son peeked in, curious. His black eyes snapped. He skittered in and rubbed against his mother, who put her arm around him, distracted by her own sad thoughts. The father came in apologetically to get his son and smiled his greeting to me.

The mother looked up and she teased her husband quietly, "My husband is different from me, you know."

"Yes," the father seemed to apologize. "I don't know why, but I cannot think about it," he explained to me. Then, again, a quick smile and he left the room.

"He doesn't want to talk about it. He doesn't want to take me to the cemetery. I go there by myself every day to be with my daughter. He says he cannot bear it," the mother explained, without blaming. I thought about the bus trip across town and the lonely hike up the hill to the cemetery, the tall cedar and hemlock, too old of a place for young children to rest.

She set her jaw with determination. Mustering up her courage, she told me, virtually a stranger, how much she hated this country at this moment, and how much she wished to be away from this town where the man who murdered her daughter lived. She spilled out her love for her daughter and her rage at this society. Before leaving that day, I promised I would come back. I asked her if she and her husband would like to visit us since I had been welcomed in her home so many times.

I wish I could remember details of the single evening they visited our home for dinner. I wish I could remember our conversation, the family stories we must have shared, what made us laugh, all the small steps we made to build a friendship. But my memories of that warm, shy, and friendly night are eclipsed by the vivid details of my final two visits.

The mother summoned me to their home. She was visibly distraught, sitting stiffly, hands clenched in her lap. "They wouldn't let me go to the trial," she began. "The police did not let me go to the trial," she said, "but I have to know. I have to know what happened to my little girl." Her dark eyes watched my face. Would I shrink? Would I stay?

"Yes, I understand," I said, sensing the urgency. I felt frustrated. "Did you know you had a right to go to the trial? Did they tell you that you have a right to face the boy who killed your daughter?"

"No," the mother said. "The police said I should not go. And my husband and friends say I should not think about it so much."

I was exasperated. How dare the police choose for her, I thought to myself. Didn't they realize the powerful effect their uniforms have upon new immigrants? Couldn't they guess the authority their opinions carried?

I felt the weight grow. The doctor who operated without informing her of all the options, the attendance clerk who did not call them at work when the young girl did not show up to school, the police officers who prevented the mother from facing her daughter's killer, a country where such violence could be done to a child, one betrayal after another, heaped on this small, steely woman, injury upon injury.

I remember her look, straight and direct into my face.

I took a deep breath. I committed myself to do whatever she needed to get through this. "I can get you the court transcript. I can bring you the words that describe how your daughter died."

"Yes," she breathed softly, and finally lowered her gaze to her lap. Her hands twisted her handkerchief. She said slowly, "That is what I would wish," and looked resolutely past me.

I felt her isolation. She told me her own people, shocked that a child could suffer such violence, found it difficult to understand the mother's actions and found it even more difficult to listen to her desperate questions and needs. The authorities, school officials, police kept a distance from her raw feelings, these professionals to whom she had entrusted the safety of her family. Her husband, of course, in his own words, did not want to talk about it. The message from all quarters seemed to be that her emotions were somehow indecent.

My husband went to the courthouse and picked up the transcript, bringing home the pages describing the crime and the court's decision. On my last visit to her home, I clutched the transcript in my hands and sat with her on the couch. I looked around for her son and her husband. They were gone. The mother sat alone, hands folded on her lap, back stiff, staring straight ahead, waiting for me to read.

I read the cold, official words. The defendant had asked the little girl to go with him to his van. He was going to show her some rabbits. There he forced her into the van, tied and blindfolded her and gagged her. He drove around town all day deciding where he would rape her. Once he passed a police car.

During the rape, the small girl was smothered and died. He rolled her in a sheet and tied her up in it, drove her to a park and dumped her body in the late afternoon.

The transcript ended there. We fell silent. I left the papers between us in case. She made no move to pick it up. Instead she grasped my hand and we held on to one another tightly, we two women, brought together in this moment of unspeakable horror. We did not let go for a long time. Then I gathered the papers and left her to her grief. She never called again.

I tried to find her later, but she and her husband had moved on to other jobs, to another place.

I would visit the young girl's grave from time to time, leaving behind some flowers or brightly wrapped hard candy. I halfway expected I might meet the mother there. Perhaps it would help a little to know that another person remembered her daughter on New Years, I thought, as I left rice cakes at the gravesite. Even today, the seven-year-old girl with the bright cheeks and black hair is always in the back of my mind, this little girl I never met except through her mother's shattered memories.

Soon after I lost track of the Laotian family, my friend Peggy contacted a center for violence against Asian Americans in Seattle who shared with her some brochures they had written in several Southeast Asian languages informing people about rape, how to protect themselves, how to report it. Through the center we learned that new immigrants, especially children, were preyed upon because violators knew there would be a good chance the rape would go unreported for two reasons. The stigma of this particular crime was high among new immigrant populations because of the sexual aspect of the violence. Beyond that, the fear of bringing the attention of authorities onto their families was even higher. New immigrants felt their immigration status was very vulnerable.

The Seattle people had some success going into the communities and educating families. However, the lack of a community center and the isolation of Asian groups from one another in our small Oregon city made this a difficult task to accomplish. Peggy and I had the bilingual brochures reprinted and made available to Southeast Asian communities, these brochures educating families to teach their children to be afraid of strangers, to run, to scream, and informing them they must report to the police. But it was too little, too late.

I have been asked since then if the crime committed against the little girl was categorized as a hate crime, if the families received social-service support, if there was a public response to their suffering. The answer to all of these questions is no. As hardworking new immigrants, balancing family and economic survival, this family had no access to support, or the knowledge of where to get it. The nearest support was in Seattle, Washington, five hours away. As for the murder being categorized a hate crime with its added penalties, this murder/rape predated any hate-crime legislation. As new immigrants, this family became pioneers in the area of violent crimes.

I have learned through the family's tragedy that one must expect that new immigrants are vulnerable to violence. In a society such as this, hate crimes are a given. That being the case, it becomes a community's responsibility to have in place a system to educate new immigrants effectively across language and culture about how to avoid victimization. Just as important, the system itself—including schools, police officers, doctors, judges—must be educated and expected to carry out its responsibilities in a just, respectful manner toward new-immigrant communities. For the newly arrived, the speakers of other languages, there should be no exceptions to the rules that are designed to protect all. No more betrayals.

Since then, I have met a young Laotian graduate student from whom I have learned about the country this family left behind. As I guessed, rape and violence toward children is unheard of in the peaceful agrarian nation of Laos. A high moral law is expected of the government and its people. According to the student, the children's access to television and other technology is consciously limited by the Laotian people through government regulations, because they wish to have control over the speed at which change takes place in their country and they do not want their cultural values interfered with like they have seen happen to their neighbors in Thailand.

She shared with me photos of robust, happy children, of schools, photos of farming and colorful celebrations in her peaceful, beautiful country. It became clearer and clearer to me why the young girl and her parents had not imagined such violence could be done against children.

Learning about Laos accentuated the sadness I felt for the family I had met so long ago. Would they ever feel safe? Will they ever feel really at home in America? I notice that their names are listed in the phone book now. I've tried several times to dial the number, but each time I try, I am overwhelmed to think that it is my voice the mother must hear whenever she remembers the details of her daughter's murder. Now, after the years have passed, I hesitate to open up those deep wounds again.

The little girl would have been a young woman by now if she had lived. If I close my eyes, I can see a small gray-haired woman, back still straight, intently watching her daughter graduate as a nurse. The father stands beside her with a gentle smile on his face, and beside him, eyes snapping, a younger brother, now a man. All three stand with such pride—in my imagination. Just as suddenly, the harsh reality interferes with the picture, a reality of a girl whose young life held her family's American dream, a girl raped and murdered, a reality of an American system that did not mete out justice, a school that did not protect the children, an immigrant community too overwhelmed by the crime to be of support.

Recently, more than ten years later, a letter to the editor of the local paper written by a young Laotian man of the same name caught my eye. He was on his way to prison. His eloquent letter took full responsibility for what he did and asked for understanding. This young man was the same little boy grown up in an immigrant family ripped apart by violence—his father choking down his lonely grief, his mother relentlessly choosing to feel its full power.

What dangers faced this little boy as he grew to be a man? What betrayals lay in store for him? In a school system with a high dropout rate among Southeast Asian students, was there a teacher or counselor who looked out for him? Both his parents probably still worked to make ends meet. Who was there at the end of the school day, he an only child with no older sister? Did this young man dare to dream as his sister had? Did he get joyful attention from parents so divided by the tragedy?

One child lost to violence. The other lost to the criminal justice system. Circumstances tore apart an American family's dream and tossed them alone into a bitter and bleak future.

9

To Serve and Protect

Terry Watada

I don't trust cops. This is not to say I dislike them as individuals. From time to time a cruiser will come down the wrong way of my one-way street in east-end Toronto and stop in the no-parking zone. The officer inside will then call out my name. I usually look up and respond with a greeting like "Hey Swamp!" or "Yo, Pig Face!" These aren't words of scorn but rather nicknames attributed back when we were together on the local high school football team. After graduating, many of my teammates went from positions on the gridiron to career positions with the city's "finest."

My enmity for the police started years before those days. When I was a kid in the 1950s, most everyone who lived in my neighborhood was "Canadian," that is, White Anglo-Saxon Protestant with a few Greeks and Italians thrown in for good measure. My family was one of two Japanese households on my street, the only people of color, but I loved hot dogs, television, and hockey. Every weekend, I played ball hockey with Ken Fleming, Frankie Johnson, and a host of other guys on the street. Makeshift goalie nets, hockey sticks bought with Christmas or birthday money, and a tennis ball were all we needed. We played for hours, envisioning Bobby Orr, Gordie Howe, and Tim Horton scoring goals and winning Stanley Cups. What could be more Canadian?

My parents were the immigrants who spoke an awkward, broken English. For my part, I hardly knew any Japanese, and my understanding of Japan came from Saturday-afternoon John Wayne movies. Outside of my parents and their friends, I considered the Japanese as the enemy. They had fought a war against us, after all. I, on the other hand, believed myself to be 100 percent Canadian. That is until the day I was shown differently.

John Fitzpatrick, a robust, husky, and larger-than-life police detective, lived on my street and was much admired. A hero to most of us. "Fitz" was a policeman, a symbol of trust, a man who lived by the motto "To Serve and Protect."

He often joined in our ball-hockey games, showing us his stick-handling techniques—his specialty was the slap shot. Among us, he favored Ken Fleming, the good-looking, blond, blue-eyed kid with athletic talents far beyond any of the rest of us. Fitz always passed him the ball, always body-checked those in the way, and always praised Ken for good play.

Fitz seemed to harbor a vague dislike of me. I was always put in net when he was playing so he could take blistering shots at me. More often than not, he would score or bruise a limb or two with his shots and then laugh at me for my ineptitude. But I didn't mind, he did it all in a joking manner. Besides, he was "Fitz."

One warm spring day we were in the neighborhood back lane playing our other favorite game: guns. Ken, Frankie, and I had out our toy rifles and machine guns, pretending to be John Wayne fighting the Japs or the Nazis, when Frankie spotted Fitz walking up the lane in his suit, overcoat, and fedora unaware of us. Ken quickly ordered us to hide behind a convenient trash can or pile of junk so that we could ambush our quarry.

When Fitz walked into our midst we jumped out, firing off our cap guns or loudly mimicking gunfire. His face froze with shock and horror. When he recovered, he reacted suddenly by grabbing me by the shirtfront and pulling out his service revolver, placing it right between my eyes.

Everything came to a screeching stop. Ken and Frankie stood frozen in their tracks. My world, my life, came down to the tiny circle of the gun barrel against my forehead.

Reeking of alcohol, he pulled me closer, still keeping the gun pressed against my skull. There was nothing but pure hatred on his face, its features distorted beyond recognition.

"So you think you got the drop on ol' Fitz," he spat, his voice quivering with adrenaline. "You little Jap. I oughta pull the trigger. I oughta for all the boys I left behind. Goddamn it I oughta." With that he let go of me and slouched up the lane, his revolver held listlessly in his hand and pointed to the ground.

That moment changed my entire life. I was told in the most certain of terms that he was not a policeman who protected the likes of me, and that somehow I was not a real Canadian, not like Ken, Frankie, or the other guys. I simply didn't belong. Thereafter, I no longer played with my friends, who anyway avoided me like I had the plague. I became a loner.

I never told my parents about what had happened. They would have told me to forget it, rise above it, walk away. My father, Matsujiro, had come from Japan when he was fourteen in 1920. Being the second son of a rice farmer, he was entitled to nothing from his father, everything going to his older brother instead. Not without compassion, my grandfather offered to take Matsujiro to a life of prosperity in Canada. He himself had been back and forth to British Columbia to work in the copper mines, on the railroad, and for the lumber camps. His son agreed, having no other option in life, and so came to Vancouver with his father and soon started working as a lumberjack. It was a strange new world to the young Matsujiro since he spoke no English. One day he happened to find himself in a greasy spoon run by a gruff, unshaven man behind the counter. When the man asked, "What'll it be, Mac?," the fresh-faced kid panicked and awkwardly pointed to a random menu item—two eggs and sausages. To his delight, the food was altogether strange and delicious. He got pretty tired of the delicacy after he had ordered it twice a day for nearly two weeks.

When my grandfather announced his return to Japan without his son, my father, still fourteen, cried out of homesickness and fear. My grandfather assured him he would be fine since he would be living and working with Japanese, eating Japanese food (when he wasn't exploring outside of Little Tokyo), and soon be returning to Japan as a rich man. My father was placated somewhat since he realized it was true: he was to be wrapped in the comfort and security of a community he understood.

My mother, Chisato Takehara, came over as a picture bride of a sort when she was eighteen. My father did indeed return to

Japan, not to stay but to get married. At twenty-seven, he was ready to start a family. My grandfather again interceded and arranged a marriage to the sixth daughter of a good friend of his, an enterprising landowner who owned a fleet of fishing boats, an extensive rice farm, and a logging company.

A grand celebration was held for the couple, with the Take-hara estate festooned in paper lanterns and the bride in a shim-mering kimono. The entire village came out to gawk and to par-take of a sumptuous feast put on by my maternal grandfather, who may have been happy to see his last daughter married off.

My mother had no choice even though she had voiced her complaint to her parents about having to live overseas in a *gai-jin*, or foreign country. She had no rights, being a woman, and to disobey her father and then her husband would have been shameful acts. By getting married, she was to lose all ties to her family and become part of my father's family.

After two weeks of marital if uneasy bliss, my father left for Canada without his bride. The government had told him to be on the next boat or be conscripted into the Japanese army and fight in Manchuria. My mother didn't see him again for two years, the Canadian government's waiting period for spouses, which suited her fine since she was sixteen and hated the idea of leaving Japan.

In Canada, the two had a hard life in the British Columbian wilderness, living in a lumber camp on a gigantic log raft that moved from site to site. Still, the money was steady, the food plentiful, and everyone they associated with was Japanese.

When the Second World War broke out, my parents were in-terned, separately at first. My father, being a Japanese national, was taken away to a road gang. In the meantime, my mother was "evacuated" to a camp in the middle of the Selkirk Moun-tains, not knowing where she was or what had happened to her husband. Eventually, he rejoined her in camp.

After the war, the couple moved to Toronto to settle in Toronto's east end. Even though they were surrounded by a "Canadian" community, they belonged to a Japanese church, maintained friendships with those from prewar B.C., and pa-tronized Japanese businesses. Only my father learned English, but in a perfunctory manner. They had come from a foreign country, had been interned and expelled from the West Coast during World War II, and in their sixties became Canadian citizens, but in their hearts they remained Japanese. As for me, I knew nothing of my parents' history at the time of the Fitz incident. Relegated to the purgatory of being neither Japanese nor Canadian, I was just angry without really knowing why.

In the decades that followed, every time I was confronted by a racist, I felt the circle of the gun barrel against my forehead and I fought back, something I hadn't done with Fitz.

And there were plenty of opportunities. Like the time an old woman called me a "gook," telling me at the same time to go back to where I came from. I spit in her face. Like the time a freshman faculty member questioned why I was in the English department. Shouldn't I be teaching the Pacific Rim to business classes? I screamed bloody murder at him in front of the assembled staff and dean. Like the time a skinhead leaned into the car I was sitting in while stopped at a red light to make a comment about "slant eyes." I punched him in the stomach when he stood up to laugh.

Fortunately for me, all was not simply "sound and fury" in my life. During the halcyon days of the 1970s when I was in university, I discovered I was woefully ignorant of my family's past. All the stories were skeletons in the closet, never to be trotted out or even referred to in any context. My parents didn't see the relevance of any of it to a nineteen-year-old seemingly happy to be engaged in the mainstream culture of rock music, cars, and dating.

Inspired by the Beatles, I had played in many Top Forty rock-and-roll bands around the city prior to university (when I didn't have to be serious about life). In the early seventies, the singer-songwriter came to the forefront of pop music, and so I decided to try my hand at songwriting, since my studies precluded my playing in a band. As with most novice writers, I decided to write about what I knew, but what did I know? So I approached my mother with the question, "How did you meet Dad?"

She hesitated at first, calling me a *baka*, or fool, for asking, but I persisted and she relented. What followed was a perception-altering revelation. My parents met through an arranged marriage! They experienced absolute poverty and hardship in British Columbia! What little they had was confiscated by the government after imprisonment and exile during and after the war! My alienation that had begun with Fitz was now complete. I finally understood that I was not a Canadian even though I lived in a country professing to be an egalitarian and tolerant state.

My rage might have turned into bitterness if not for the fact that I remembered my original impulse in asking my mother about her life. I wrote a song. In his review of my discography for the first issue of *Rice Paper*, a magazine produced by the Asian Canadian Writers Workshop, Kuan Foo said, "Nowhere is the loss [of tradition and identity] felt more acutely than in 'New Denver,' the album's simplest song and its centrepiece. Here Watada strips away all metaphor and poetic license and tells the story of internment through the eyes of two internees who fell in love in the New Denver prison camp." He quoted lines from my song:

The government took all my property but I'll survive somehow.
And all I can offer you is a lifetime of hardships my love.
Maybe love's not worth much in these troubled times,
But it's the only thing we can live on, on the outside, in the snow.

At about the time I wrote that song, the Asian American political/cultural movement was in full flight. Alan Hotta, editor of *The New Canadian*, a Japanese Canadian community newspaper located in Toronto, called me after I submitted the lyrics to "New Denver" for publication and asked me to join in a "rap session" with other Asian Canadians to discuss the various issues within the community. In the years that followed I was introduced to the writings of Black activists like Malcolm X, Eldridge Cleaver, and LeRoi Jones. I also listened to the music of Chris Iijima, Joanne Miyamoto, and "Charlie" Chin, which surprised and inspired me since here were other Asians writing songs about living in America. I no longer felt alone.

I continued to write and perform my music (six albums' worth) all over North America. I met like-minded people everywhere. Fellow artists like "Charlie" Chin, Maxine Hong Kingston, Joy Kogawa, Roy Kiyooka, Sky Lee, Lane Nishikawa, Number One Son, David Henry Hwang, John Seetoo, and others helped shape my own artistic endeavors.

During the 1980s, I turned my efforts toward the redress campaigns in North America. Playing venues—anything from a formal concert auditorium to a church hall—in Vancouver, Vernon, Winnipeg, Toronto, Hamilton, and Montreal in Canada, and San Francisco, Oakland, Chicago, Lansing, Oberlin, and New York City in the United States, I met dozens more Asian North Americans and took in the spirit of community and the strength of a just cause to nourish my soul.

In 1988, redress was settled in both countries. For me, the apology and the gesture of compensation weren't enough for the years of suffering endured by my parents (both had passed away before the announcement) and my community, but I once again felt like a true Canadian. Many injustices had been committed, but I knew then that anyone could stand up for his or her rights and be heard.

Since the 1980s and into the new millennium, racism hasn't subsided; in fact, it has intensified. At the same time, there has been a marked increase in hate crimes. The rise of the two isn't just coincidence.

In the mid-1980s, the Ku Klux Klan, it was discovered, had infiltrated various high schools in Toronto. They had started "social clubs" to recruit the weak-minded and insecure to further their crusade of hate. The Western Guard, the long-standing Canadian White-supremacist group, also made inroads among adolescents.

The hue and cry was loud and sustained among educators, social workers, civic politicians, and activists. Action was taken to get these groups out of the schools, but their influence wasn't eradicated.

Outside covens were established. The Internet gave these groups and neo-Nazi groups all over North America a new pulpit from which to spread their "gospel." Hate came into the home through the personal computer.

In the late 1980s and early 1990s, skinheads began appearing on Toronto's downtown streets, some as "squeegee kids," most as layabouts and miscreants. With their cries of "White is right!" accompanied by obscene and racist gesticulations, the influence of the KKK and their ilk was obvious. They constituted a malevolent presence, their anger as well as their sense of power palpable to passersby. Who else but a hateful and self-assured individual would walk up to a stranger's car and stick his head inside to blast the occupant for being a "slant eye"?

In 1990, all the pent-up emotions exploded when Tony Le, a fifteen-year-old high school student, and Mukesh Nararyan, his friend, were knifed to death among the glittering lights and brand-name neon of Yonge Street, Toronto's Fifth Avenue. A group of skinheads had decided they didn't like "foreign garbage" littering the streets.

I was outraged by the murders, not only because two innocent Asian kids had lost their lives out of ignorance and the rot of hate but for the relative inaction by the police to prevent such incidents. Emboldened by the success of the redress campaign, I continued to write music as well as poems, stories, and plays, all with an eye to bringing to light the issues that directly affect the Asian North American communities and plague society in general.

The case of the police is one such issue.

Toronto has recently begun to live up to its boast of being "a world-class city." The city's population has evolved from the homogeneity of the 1950s to the vital mix of races and cultures it is today. Neighborhoods have become ethnic enclaves that go beyond the tawdry tourist trap: Greek Town, Chinatown (five and counting), Korea Town, Little Italy, and Little India serve their communities well. On any given day, there is a verbal soup of syllables, accents, and dialects on the subways. The demographics of the city may have changed, but unfortunately not the police in finding ways to meet the challenges of such a diverse population.

Every now and then, the Police Services Board (a citizens' watchdog committee) recommends that the Metropolitan Toronto Police Department recruit visible minorities. And they do: Sikh police officers are allowed to wear turbans, the height restrictions have been removed to allow Asians to join the police force, and officers of a particular ethnic background are assigned to their community. But these are seen as cosmetic changes used for promotion rather than a real attempt at diversity. The vast majority of the force is still White.

When taking that into account, as well as the number of killings by the police in the past five years alone, a disturbing trend emerges. Tommy Barnett was shot four times from thirty-six to forty-five inches away. Andrew Bramwell was shot three times by police in the lower back. Wayne Williams:

hit in the chest and neck by four of seven shots fired. Edmond Yu: killed by three of six shots fired from six to seven feet away. Huge Dawson: struck by eleven bullets. And Xie Pei Yang: shot in the heart. On New Year's Eve, 1999, Henry Masuka was shot to death when officers fired five times in the emergency ward of St. Michael's Hospital, where he was seeking treatment for his son. In each case, the victim was either African Canadian or Asian Canadian, and in each case, no charges were laid, except against one of the officers who fired on Huge Dawson. He was charged with manslaughter, but no conviction was handed down. Instead, the Police Association (the police union) accused the Special Investigations Unit of mounting a witch hunt.

Granted, in Edmond Yu's case, the three police officers were confronted by a schizophrenic off his medication, homeless, and wielding a weapon (a silver pocket hammer), but the very severity of the response borders on cruelty, even calculation. Why is the first response also the last response, especially when dealing with people of color? What are they thinking when it comes to victims like Tony Le and Mukesh Nararyan? Do they care at all? Are they allowing or even committing hate crimes rather than preventing them? Are they no better than the skinheads? What does the motto "To Serve and Protect," so proudly emblazoned on their arm patches and cruiser doors, truly mean?

Given my cynicism brought about by Fitz, my parents' experience in Canada, and my years of political struggle, everything seems to boil down to that one question: whom do the police really serve and protect?

In reaction to the Edmond Yu incident, I wrote *Vincent*, a play about the violent end of a schizophrenic outpatient at the hands of the police. It garnered much attention and praise, even from the police department's hierarchy. The play still tours as a constant reminder that the police motto is meant to include the mentally ill and in a broader sense all Canadians—no matter the color, the ethnic background. Unfortunately, the police have only paid lip service to the concerned and angry voices demanding diversity in the force and change in enforcement policies.

I haven't come across the virulent hate of a drunken Fitz of late, but the aforementioned killings, the subsequent inaction of the department, and the controversy of the Police Association's recent scheme (cleverly called the "True Blue Campaign") to create a slush fund through telephone solicitation in order to conduct investigations and smear campaigns against politicians who are perceived as a threat have led me to an all too obvious answer: as in the past, they serve and protect themselves and their own kind.

10

🌀

My Noose

Doug A. Tang

It is the rope shaped like life itself, shaped like a drop of water. Strange fruit grows from this rope, and this rope grows down from the branches of trees. But the rope itself is no fruit of the tree. It is the fruit of human beings. The rope is called a noose. The strange fruit, as Billie Holiday calls them, are usually men, men of the other color, of the other race or religion. Those others are often Black, sometimes brown, and more often than Americans will admit, yellow-skinned Asiatic men.

Most of the history is lost. Probably because most of the hangings of the Chinamen and the other yellow bastards were done out West, in the 1800s and early 1900s, in small towns, and as a matter of extermination and probably not as a great sport or symbol of Southern White superiority. The Chinamen were rats. Rats scurrying away with gold and jobs. We needed exterminating. We were tools, tools that outlasted their usefulness and needed to be thrown away. When I worked as a community organizer for the United Farm Workers union, legendary organizer Dolores Huerta pointed out to me a place in Salinas, California, where twelve Chinese farmworkers had been hung. The means to an end had demanded more money or refused to work or something.

I had never heard about this mass hanging even though I had done extensive research on anti-Asian violence for my master's thesis. No matter what white sheets America throws over the truth, the noose, as much as to another group of people in this country, belongs to the Chinaman. It is our gift, and we have taken it, throughout our history in this nation, with our own clanging discord, which to White America has sounded like harmless Chinaman music. I wish I had tried on the noose, not to hang myself, but just to see how it felt.

I had the opportunity when I was about twelve. I woke up one Sunday morning, threw open the curtains, and looked outside at the spring, and there it was, hanging from that ash tree directly in front of my window. It was about fifteen feet away, and I didn't have my glasses on, and to most any other kid it would have looked like a rope for hanging potted plants, and my mom had plenty of those. But I had grown up there, in College Station, Texas, and for most of my years had been the only Chinese kid in my grade. I was one of only a few in the area at all, and I knew how things were. I figured that if it looked like a noose, it probably was a noose. I put on my glasses, went outside, and looked at it. It was on a low branch, and it was a rather thin rope, and I could look straight through the hole. It was made for me.

Before there was telemarketing or caller ID, there were the phone calls. I don't know when it started. From what my parents tell me, it started before I was born in 1970. And in 1999, my parents told me that they had not received any "bad calls" for a couple of years. Many of the calls were racist or obscene. Most of the calls were silent. My mother, father, me, or my sister would pick up the phone at any time during the day or night and say, "Hello? Hello? Hello? Hello? Hello?" until we realized that whoever was on the other line was not going to speak. And yet whoever that person was, he or she would not hang up either. The gift to us was silence.

Over the years, we got used to the calls, which, during their height, might come a few times each day. And to this day, it still happens sometimes, and it makes me ill to hear my parents say "hello" too many times as they greet the silence. Sometimes, I wish that during the later years we had gotten caller ID and found out who these people were. I wish I had gone to their homes to see them and listen to them give me silence to my face.

And then there were the words. At school, beginning from kindergarten and lasting through the twelfth grade, I was treated to the ching-chong songs, the Chinese Japanese dirty knees look at these rhymes, the Chinks, gooks, Japs, the sure is getting nippy in here, ain't it?, the you eat dog, yo mama eat dogs, your greasy greasy grandma eats dogs, the do you know karate?, if I hit you, are you going to use kung fu on me?, why did you bomb Pearl Harbor?, commie, red Chinese, my daddy killed you in Vietnam, didn't I see you on *M*A*S*H*, the bow with the hands together, the waaaaahh with the kung fu kick ah you in tha butt aahhh soooo!, and all those songs that snuggle so well within the American harmony.

In college at Texas A&M, I was called a Vietcong a couple of times, mostly for being Asian and left wing. As a substitute teacher in Austin, the kids would not hesitate to do the same things that kids did to me when I was a student in school, except this time I was in charge; so I sent these White, Black, and Latino kids to the office. The schools were so bad that sometimes even before class started, I would write on the board that racial epithets would be punished by an automatic referral to the office. But everyone knows that it is sticks and stones that break bones. The actual violence maintained against me must be categorized in years, and not separate incidents. The boys (who would be boys) hit me in the arms, chest, back, and head, slapped me, kicked me, shoved me, twisted my fingers around, twisted my arms, took advantage of flag football, or any sport, by tackling me, threw my stuff away, lifted me by the collar and throat, all the while threatening me, insulting me, and spitting on me. They did it in groups of two or three, or with their friends or supporters around. Sometimes a certain pair of boys would terrorize me during and after school for months in a row. Sometimes they would stalk me and wallop me from behind. I caught hell from mostly Whites, but also Latinos and Blacks. I never got my ass kicked. I never got the crap kicked out of me. I never had my face rearranged.

Of the thousands of opportunities I had to get into a fight, I refused almost every single time. I believed in the Gandhian philosophy of nonviolence. Around the age of ten, I watched the movie *Gandhi*, and I had found the way. Also, from a very young age, I had been taught that fighting was wrong. And finally, even at a very young age, I had a sense of how to live with dignity. Yeah. I came up with a whole lot of baloney in order to keep from being beaten up.

Many Asian American boys and men have died from being beaten by racists. It is something often excused as "boys being boys," but it should not be. Nevertheless, I wish I had been a "boy." I wish I would have gotten my ass kicked at an early age, maybe eight or nine, just to know what it felt like. Just to know that I could survive it. If I had not survived it, I would not have been around to worry about it anymore, and if I had suffered some permanent spinal injury, they would have trouble picking on a kid in a wheelchair. Had any one of those three possibilities occurred, there would have been a certain closure, and I would have had the experience of being beaten and humiliated securely under my belt.

Instead, the unknowns got to me. The unknown of who tied the noose to the tree. The unknown of who kept calling our house with either racist commentaries or silence. And the unknown of what it would be like if they finally got me or took me away. By the time I was fourteen, the lack of knowledge, the omission of Hard Facts, led me to often wonder who was watching me, who was tracking us, what did they want? Each time something bad happened, I tried to figure it into the larger conspiracy of phone calls, violence, and general racism. It seemed possible that someone was watching me as I went to sleep, that they could be hanging another noose as I slumbered.

Racism crossed adolescent male sexuality and gave birth to paranoia fueled by the shame associated with sex acts. I came to believe that "They" were watching as I masturbated in my bed. It occurred to me during these times that I could be the shame of my family, the laughingstock of my school. In high school, I began almost always wrongly accusing friends and enemies of spying on me, connecting them with both real acts of racism/vandalism and acts that I made up myself. I asked if they were working with others, spreading the news about me to others. Others. More and more others came into being.

When I got into college, I understood the larger conspiracies around me as incorporating the government, the CIA, my parents, my girlfriends, and all my enemies and friends. It continued throughout college and graduate school, even though I had realized by the age of eighteen that there might be something wrong with my way of thinking. But the problem with paranoia, at least my problem with it, is that you're never quite sure.

Maybe it's me. Maybe it's reality. Maybe it's both. Paraphrasing former Israeli Prime Minister Golda Meier, just because I'm paranoid doesn't mean you're not out to get me.

In addition to my conspiratorial view of the world, I also saw a more realistic parallel world. This world contained a readily fixable humanity, one massive glob of people who were essentially the same on the inside, and who simply needed to be made "aware" of the actual reality (which I, even with my alternate visions, claimed to see clearly). In this world, the people, after being enlightened about oppression and racism, would all shake each other's hands and say "Peace be with you." Along with this world came a structure of meaning and purpose; my life-purpose was to help get rid of oppression and racism. I could and would help save the world.

In college at Texas A&M University, I became by default the president of a campus organization called Students Against Apartheid (SAA), which was part of the worldwide effort to abolish the system of racial oppression in South Africa known as apartheid. Every semester, SAA would build a shanty on the main campus. The shanty represented both the living conditions of the typical Black South African and the moral poverty of apartheid and racism. Every semester that the shanty was built, some students or residents or who knows who would tear the shanty down, or spray-paint "KKK" and "White Power" on it, or do something more creative like hang dead pigeons from its ceiling. In addition to educating some portion of humanity about apartheid, I wrote a consistently left-wing column for the school newspaper. And I was the de facto leader of an organization known as the Medicine Tribe.

I became a notorious figure at politically conservative Texas A&M, a wanted man, someone who received threatening phone calls and was listed on supposedly mock hit lists. Of course, all of the overt acts against me only made my vision of the covert organizations explode in enormity and complexity.

I graduated from Texas A&M in 1992, and beginning in January 1993, I worked for six months as a community organizer for the United Farm Workers. I spent ten weeks in Phoenix, often working on the campus of Arizona State University in nearby Tempe. In the spring of 1993, a Chinese ASU graduate student was knocked from his bike by two men and beaten unconscious.

The assailants did not take his wallet or his bike. He required metal reinforcements to reconstruct his face. The police immediately ruled out the possibility of the assault being a hate crime, and the Tempe police did not even further investigate the crime until the Asian American community pressured them to do so. I got involved with the community-organizing efforts to reeducate the Tempe Police Department on hate crimes and the Asian American community.

When I finished my work with the farm workers, having helped to organize the funeral of Cesar Chavez (who had died in April 1993), I returned to Texas and entered the Asian Studies master's program at the University of Texas in Austin. The department allowed me to write a thesis about Asian Americans, and I decided to write my thesis on the history of the politics surrounding cases of anti-Asian violence in the United States. In my case studies, I documented the attack at ASU, the subsequent community organizing, and the improved police and community cooperation in the aftermath of a second attack, on another Chinese graduate student, which occurred about a year after the first attack. Upon submitting my thesis, I believed that if policemen were trained and communities kept vigilant, anti-Asian hate crimes would be handled correctly. Through the keeping of proper books and statistics, and through the publicizing of hate crimes and hate-crimes statistics (the Hate Crimes Statistics Act having been made law in 1992), I believed that the frequency of anti-Asian violence would somehow substantially diminish.

During my last year of graduate study, in 1995, I cosprouted a movement to establish an Asian American Studies program at UT Austin. This movement eventually succeeded, and as of the year 2000 students may now earn a bachelor's degree in Asian American Studies. The university has thus far hired two permanent faculty members dedicated to the program and plans to hire more in the future. The College of Liberal Arts, however, has not yet made the commitment of hiring a permanent director. Perhaps my central inspiration for working for this movement was to help educate people on the complex, human history and nature of Asian America so that fewer hate crimes might occur against us. The establishment of an Asian American Studies department will do more to prevent anti-Asian violence than a hundred theses could.

During the first twenty-five years of my life, my heart was tightly wrapped around a warm and fuzzy core that kept my life meaningful and made me feel like a dignified man. That core was the philosophy of nonviolence. In this, my version of the nonviolent philosophy of King and Gandhi, my own desire to tear the throats out of my tormentors was a weakness that I should never give into. It was like my original sin, my evil nature. In the sixth grade, two boys grabbed me, and one had his hand over my face and the other was going to do something bad. I had just watched *Gandhi* (the movie) and I was reading his biography. But I didn't know what that other kid was going to do to me. I didn't want to have him spit in my ear and have it get reinfected, with green stuff coming out of it again. I did not want to be humiliated in front of the whole class and in front of that cute country girl Debbie Dunham, who said she liked me. I didn't think she was kidding. So I punched out, and punched out, and punched away. And I hit something or someone. They stopped, and my fist was all scraped up.

The social studies teacher (of course a coach) demanded that we sit down and do our work. I began drawing pictures of myself blasting big holes in the heads of my tormentors, stabbing them, and dismembering them. When the two boys asked me what I was drawing, I told them. They apologized for their actions. It was the only time my racist cohorts ever apologized to me.

I went to my next class—English—and I told my friend why I was crying, about how I had to hit someone, about how I had done the thing I didn't want to do. He was a good Christian White boy, and he acted like he understood. But when I devised a plan the next year for us to ambush the football player who was punching me in the head during our life sciences class, the good Christian boy of course simply could not identify with such silly schemes. I was supposed to turn the other cheek. Which is exactly what I wished I could do. Oh, yes, even though Jesus was not my friend, I still believed. I believed, I believed, Lord knows I believed in nonviolence. What I really wanted to do was kill them. No matter how much you tell yourself that you believe in nonviolence, you can only control your emotions so much. Denial may be the only tool when dealing with the primal urge to destroy those males of your species who have disre-

Doug A. Tang

spected you. We are animals. We are born from animals, not from moral formulas or the holy heavens. Throughout my childhood, and even into my adult life, I regretted not taking advantage of opportunities for successful retaliation.

I was eight when our family moved to a dead-end street of mostly upper-middle-class families. Soon after we arrived, I was welcomed to the street by a White boy on a bike deriding the Chinese language. I was practicing hitting with a baseball and a bat when he rode by, singing. I stood paralyzed. I could have easily surprised him and run up to him and knocked him off the bike with the bat. And then, as I imagined for years afterward, I would have worked his flesh and bones over with American hardwood.

Thus began my love affair with hatred and violence. It outlasted my torrid romance with the philosophy of nonviolence, which ended with a fist being slammed into the passenger-side window of my car, and the screaming of, "Fuckin' gooks! Fuck you, you fuckin' gooks!" In 1995, my girlfriend was Chinese, and her name was Jane. We were stopped at an intersection on the west side of the University of Texas. She was in the passenger seat. She was in shock. The young racist ran off with his friends. I drove around the block. I told her I was going to run them over. As I got back to the street, I spotted them running and riding skateboards along the commercial strip. There were other cars parked along the curb, and I could not get to them. We went back to my apartment, and I threw a plank with nails through the end of it into the back of the car. Next time, I would nail them. I went upstairs and stared. I had not even had the chance to give them the hateful glare, which I had projected all my life onto all who would humiliate me. As my girlfriend prepared for bed, I played a tape of the clanging abscess of notes that is Thelonius Monk's "Round Midnight," played solo by Thelonius. The loneliest.

Texas governor George W. Bush had recently passed a law allowing for registered concealed weapons. I wanted more than anything else to take advantage of this law and "defend" myself. As I felt the catharsis of blue dissonance wash over me, I began to realize that the one who hates the most in the tango of hate crimes is the victim. While the hate criminal skates away the night and maybe throws things at people or spray paints a wall,

I think about what caliber bullet will make the biggest hole in his chest. I cannot recall whether it was before or after this revelation that a Vietnamese freshman at UT Austin, a smart student, pierced the skull of a fellow student with a .22-caliber bullet. The shot killed the Latino student. The Vietnamese kid got two ninety-nine-year sentences, to be served consecutively. However much sadness I felt for this Latino kid, I also knew the Vietnamese kid's story. At least I knew what it could be. He had grown up in Texas; if he had had a childhood similar to mine, then he had learned to hate at an early age. Hatred is the gift that is poured into the Asian American soul from birth, and poured in like molten American steel. And just like steel, it hardens within us, and is impossible to dislodge without suicide. For Asian America, hate is the price of pride. When the Latino kid slighted the Vietnamese kid and his friends, death was the price of hate.

I had been fooling myself for a long time. When one has such a severe split between one's philosophy of right and wrong and one's heart's desires, one tries to maintain a wide gulf between the two, trying to confine them to different departments in one's life. For instance, one's violent desires may be confined to one's fantasy life, while one's moral philosophy is applied rigorously to one's public, active life. For me, the two began mixing it up with each other like grimy mud wrestlers. Even as I worked for Cesar Chavez, a famous advocate of nonviolence, I had come up with a theory of political activism: to achieve a political goal (especially as a grassroots activist), one must choose one's political target (a politician or bureaucrat), and through whatever acceptable tactics one must make that person suffer an ulcer or a heart attack. With such a chink in the armor of nonviolent philosophy, anything is possible. Eventually, I was making cryptic threats to radio disc jockeys who made racist comments against Asians, believing that my ends justified my means. A big part of me still believes that in many cases, threats, psychological warfare, and generally playing with the enemy's emotions are acceptable means to fight racism—whose means and ends are often deadly.

During the 1990s, I talked to dozens of people about their experiences growing up Asian in America. Most of these people grew up outside of California and Hawaii. I learned of Asian American experiences that were worse than mine, and childhoods that were better. I learned of a Chinese American woman who had required years of therapy to work out the humiliating acts imposed upon her (like being stuffed into a locker). I learned of a Mongolian American man who had been a great student and a happy child before he moved to Indiana. After fighting racists (and putting many into the hospital) on a regular basis for years, the experience left him mentally unstable. He is now homeless. I met men who, in my position, decided to get into the fights that would have reduced my torture by years. I met other men who tried to take it like a man, as boys. What sickened me most was that the people I talked to suffered most of their racist verbal and physical attacks at or around school. Worse yet was the prevalence and consistency of the experiences. What varied the most was how Asian Americans internalized (or kept external) and processed the hate and violence. Some were able to brush it off. Others held resentment and anger. Yet others it crushed.

If my world treats me like a dog, perhaps I start becoming a dog, thinking that I am a dog and acting like one. None of us are immune to the environment we live in, and especially the environment we grow up in. With a huge proportion of Asian America having grown up among often violent racism, has our whole ethnic group acquired certain traits or characteristics as a result? I am especially interested in what the consistent physical harassment has done to Asian American men. Has it somehow stunted our masculinity, or rather, our maturity as men?

Let us take my case for example. I learned what it meant to be a man not only from my father and mother but also from the Texan and Southern teachers, parents, old people, friends, and enemies among whom I grew up. Being a man, it seemed to me, had a lot to do with the ability to both withstand and commit violence. Being a man means being smooth and successful with the ladies. Masculinity, according to gender academicians, is not something that one gains at birth; it is something that men and boys must prove over and over again to maintain their own sense of penis possession. But growing up as a dog in a world of boys and girls, I was taught by the other boys that I was not tough; however "mature" it may have been to avoid violence and simply "express my feelings" by giving the glare, the world told me deep down inside that I was no man. And in part because I was stereotyped by my peers as a brain with no body and no genitals, I felt that I never had a chance with the ladies, so I never really tried. Having these two main components of my young understanding of masculinity denied, my mind became preoccupied with being such a man for years after adolescence. As others were learning of other forms of masculinity, like excelling in one's career or raising a family, my development was arrested and thrown in the prison of my own glands.

These days, at twenty-nine, I often try to make myself absorb a different idea of masculinity, one that is more traditionally Chinese—one that involves serving my family and starting one of my own. Of course my case is only one case. Exactly how has Asian America been transformed by the crucible of racism and anti-Asian violence? Has the development of our masculinity been arrested? What evidence do we have?

The national equivalent of schoolyard race-taunting occurred when 2000 presidential candidate John McCain called his Vietnamese captors during the Vietnam War "gooks" over and over again for the national media to hear. After weeks of his using the epithet, some national media finally reported it. Did we wipe the spit off our faces and fight? I learned of only one rather anemic protest, which occurred at McCain's rally in Little Saigon (Riverside, California). At this protest, young Asians wore shirts with "American Gook" scrawled across the chests. Many of the older Vietnamese Americans at the rally, who supported McCain and rationalized his statements, kicked and spat at the younger protestors, calling them communists. But what speaks loudest to me is the resolute silence of the rest of Asian America. We have the taste of bile and excrement in our mouths from childhoods and adulthoods peppered with racism. Is that why so many of us men seek the security of computer monitors and professional offices? Non-Asians ask me where our Jesse Jackson is. I don't know, but I'm sure we could program a virtual Jesse.

I moved to Los Angeles in 1997 to improve my fiction and screenwriting skills by earning my masters of professional writing from the University of Southern California. By working with an Asian American nonprofit media organization, I perfected my screenplay, *Jaundice*. *Jaundice* is about the evolution of an Asian American man from young patriot and follower of Martin Luther King's dream into a violent vigilante. He grows up with one Black and one White boy, and when they reach adulthood, their struggles in their small town for lives of dignity puts them in deadly conflict with each other. After one of these men kills his father, the Asian finally picks up his own pistols. Although my move to L.A. was good for my writing career (we are now seeking financing for the film), I went there while struggling with serious personal problems. Among my panoply of personal issues was a deep and dedicated self-loathing. My isolation in the city of angels—those beautiful implant-enhanced angels—put me in the psychologist's office more than once. I didn't realize it then, but I was trying to kill myself by sleep deprivation and by absentmindedly driving through red lights. When I went to the shrink's office, they took the *DSM IV* off the shelf and diagnosed me with the entire book. Anxiety, depression, paranoia, borderline personality disorder, even "schizoaffective" symptoms (whatever that means).

My mental illness worsened during the 1998–1999 school year. In an age when people can claim the ability to make and remake themselves, the number of images, commercials, and media "programs" that tell us who we are and what we should be, and—just as importantly—who and what others are, has increased exponentially. These de facto media suggestions have infiltrated our computers, our work, our school, even our spirituality.

These images and programs are a hundred times bigger, louder, and uglier in Los Angeles, which is fine if one keeps one's head above the corporate culture's floodwaters. But Los Angeles is like a blond, dumb succubus; she looks so innocuous upon approach, so easily containable in her obvious superficiality. But once you enter her, you are seduced. You need more money, you need smoother skin, a prettier face, stronger muscles, a faster car, a higher rung on the ladder, you need more power in every way. Again, I lumped humanity together. We were all indeed the same inside, I thought, and we all wanted the same things: supreme power, ultimate highs, and otherworldly orgasms. And in Los Angeles, it seemed to me that people, who were all the same, all looked for the same things in the same places: in the manipulation of physical bodies, in appearances, in superficialities, in material wealth and symbols, and in seeing oneself as superior to (all) others.

In a lot of ways, my life has been one crisis of masculinity after another. Soaking in Hollywoodworld, I looked at all the weak

Asian American men and all the strong other kinda men. Even the rise of stars like Jackie Chan, Jet Li, and Chow Yun Fat made me more loathing of Asian men, because I knew that few Asian men were like that. I did not bother to see that neither were all other kinda men really like their hyped-up media images. While I myself have had few problems attracting women, it seemed to me that the general rule was that Asian men were undesirable. I assumed that there was something wrong with us. I assumed that what I had been told all my life was actually true: I ain't nothing but a ching-chong Chinkie Chinaman. For a long time, I teetered between believing that the problem was me and believing that I was the exception: all the other Asian men were the problem, and unfortunately, I was lumped in with the rest of those bastards. Much of my denigration of the Asian American male had to do with our seeming to be neither a "man's man" nor a "ladies' man"; the dignity and honor that define the masculinity of most Asian men was completely invisible to me.

Months of obsessing over the Asian male led me to want to exterminate all of us. My desire was visceral; I could feel it in my trigger finger. I reminded myself of Hitler, whose mother was Jewish, making him a Jew as well. This fantasy of self-genocide brings us up to the present and back to the subject of this essay: anti-Asian violence. The sick beauty of hate crimes and racism is that the perpetrator gets to play the role of their Christian God. They get to remake their victims in their own image. Growing up, others hit me because I was an Asian male. After years of such pounding, I learned eventually to want to hit Asian men, too. I eventually emerged from this self-genocidal state of mind around the beginning of the year 2000. It's May 2000 right now.

Almost thirty years old now, I often wonder what happened to my noose, the one I touched about twenty years ago. The rope that looks like life itself. I can't help but believe inside my soul that this life is meant for me. We were all women and men before we were members of any ethnicity. I have learned from my own violent desires that anti-Asian violence occurs when the distorted face of Asian America crosses the primal need for masculine expression and confirmation. I have learned from my tormentors that anti-Asian violence is not necessarily a hate crime. One does not necessarily hate the dog one kicks or the rat one stomps on. One needs only disdain or disregard him for his ethnicity.

We are the tools, the objects, the living punching bags of millions of power trips, sadistic highs, and ego-boosting sessions throughout the country. The opposite of masculinity is not necessarily femininity, but something that is not human. Different cultures have different definitions of what a real man is, but all of them share the same disgust at a man who is not a man. When a man doubts his own masculinity or when he believes that others doubt it, he must prove it, and do so as many times as possible. If he sees in himself weakness, cowardice, dishonor, failure in his social role, stupidity or incoherence, clumsiness, or flaming homosexuality, he will seek to destroy it. He may do so in various ways. One way is to defeat another man. The less human that other man seems, the more of a threat to his masculinity and/or the more of a symbol of what he hates in himself, then the more the first man will try to defeat, harm, or kill that other man. I know this from watching myself and my racist enemies.

Asian America is largely a faceless glob of humanity. Collectively, we constitute the Rosencrantz and Guildenstern of the ongoing American tragedy (except that on the *Late Night with David Letterman* our names are Mujibur and Sirajul). When Rosencrantz and Guildenstern die in *Hamlet*, the show goes on without a skip in the rhythm. As minor characters meant to die in service of the central drama, we are easily caricaturized for the sake of guffaws, or vilified for dark contrast, or fetishized to twitch the libido. Our roles in America are cast like shadows; we are the foils resulting from the spotlight being shined on the main players.

Tired of being kicked around, some of us wish to become the kickers. So we try to become what we think our oppressors are like, not knowing that we are destroying ourselves in the process, and raising them to the position of gods, gods whose characteristics we have created partially out of the awe and despising of the consistently victimized. Some of us think that if we make enough money or contribute enough to the Democratic and Republican parties, we will buy respect. Yet others hope that we can simply withdraw further into the shadows. But we are the shadows, and our faces will be painted and dragged out whenever we are needed for shadowboxing.

Asian America must come together as a nation. As an Asian American nation, we must prop each other up, not just as Asians, but also as men and women, as store owners and retail workers, as old people and young people, as disabled citizens and professional athletes, and as actors and sorely honest writers. But never as dogs and rats. We must stop our own anti-Asian disdain, dehumanization, and violence in order to stop theirs. As a creator of media (a writer and would-be screenwriter), I see that the corporate capitalist structure tends to promote particular types of Asian Americans and Asian American stories. In the animal sense, we are allowed to be prey and predators. In the gender sense, we are being separated from each other; when was the last time you saw an Asian American man and an Asian American woman kiss in the movies?

As I have stated before, we are human animals, men and women, before we are Asian. We must re-produce our images, our voices, and our stories as human male and female selves in order to be fully respected by others and ourselves as Human Beings with Asian Faces. With the amount of excess capital available to Asian America (because of the high number of wealthy Asians), we must invest in and support our own film- and TV-production companies, publishing companies, and music-recording companies and distributors. Wealthy and powerful Asian Americans especially should take it upon themselves to share their wealth in order to uplift Asian America from our current state of constant humiliation within the mass media.

On another point, Asian Americans must look inside themselves, and if they find a disdain for other Asian Americans, they must ask themselves why. Our current doormat status in America is a reflection of both the large number of feet ready to step on us and our willingness to put ourselves and our fellow Asian Americans down at the feet of the rest of the country. We must remake ourselves in our own individual minds before a social mind-set can begin to reverberate outward and shake awake the whole of America, so that America may see us standing on central stage, not as shadows, but as stars in our own right. Through self-examination, politics, education, arts, media, and the proper use of economic power, we must remake ourselves in our own image, as living, breathing, complete, and beautiful men and women—as human animals, proud, powerful, and alive with dignity.

IV

⑤

EPILOGUE AND
AFTERWORD

Epilogue

P. W. Hall

For many years now, I have studied the histories of the Asian Americans, Jews, and African Americans. In addition to making connections between the personal and social dynamics of hate crimes, it is crucial that we examine connections between all racial and ethnic groups, in various time periods, who have been targets of hate crimes. This is particularly pressing since the perpetrators are often the same. The crimes of the neo-Nazis, for example, beg this sort of comparative analysis. While it is certainly not productive to engage in comparisons of the quantity of suffering among victims, it is indeed important to note underlying ideological, psychological, and sociological similarities. Underlying the hatred of both the Nazis in Europe (especially during the Holocaust of the 1940s) and the neo-Nazis today is their supremacist desire for an all-White world and their genocidal mentality. In this regard, the Nazi mind-set has not changed much in the past fifty years. How can we begin to understand that common mentality, as well as corresponding similarities in the experiences of victims?

Let's begin by examining the relationship between the oppressor and the oppressed. In his classic volume, *Pedagogy of the Oppressed*, Paulo Freire examines the oppressive mentality: "the oppressor . . . is himself dehumanized because he dehumanizes others" (29); "[f]or the oppressors, 'human beings' refers only to

171

themselves; other people are 'things'" (39); "[v]iolence is initiated by those who oppress, who exploit, who fail to recognize others as persons" (37).

The vision of the oppressor is dominated by stereotypes, and these false images, rather than the social or individual reality of other human beings, determine his or her actions. This is a recurring theme in this book. As Eric Mar has described, Mr. Kao was shot because the police incorrectly stereotyped him as a kung fu expert. The police had failed to see Mr. Kao as a human being: what they saw instead was a false stereotype. They mistakenly believed that all Asians were martial-arts experts when they said that Kao was wielding a stick. Yet a search of his house for martial arts weapons was in vain; they found none. In reality, very few Asians actually know kung fu. Because Kao was dehumanized and caricatured in the minds of the police, he lost his life.

Freire also emphasizes that both the oppressed and the oppressor lose their humanity when acts of racism, racial violence, or oppression are committed. This dehumanization process is common in the military. During wartime, soldiers are often taught to dehumanize their enemies, thereby making it easier for them to kill. This is how Hitler effected the murders of Jews, Gypsies, homosexuals, and others defined as subhuman during World War II. Since the 1920s, the Chinese and Japanese have been negatively stereotyped, caricatured, and made to look evil in posters (Chan 44), which has made it easier for Western military forces to kill them. During times of economic tension, Asian Americans have been blamed and penalized on the labor market, as well as blamed for a slew of other social problems. These trends are similar to the experience of Jews prior to the escalation of the Holocaust, and the similarities are important to understand. Racial violence can have the effect of deadening the soul of its victims. Hate crimes are immoral acts of violence. What is lost in all of this, says Freire, is the humanity of both the oppressed and the oppressors.

In the face of this oppressive mentality, Freire places special importance on the perspective of the oppressed for social understanding. He writes, "Who are better prepared than the oppressed to understand the terrible significance of an oppressive society? Who suffer the effects of oppression more than the oppressed?" (27). Certainly, those who have actually experienced racism or hate crimes are best able to define oppression. Hence the significance of this collection of writings by Asian Americans. They write about the process of experiencing oppression, struggling to understand it, working to transform and regain their own sense of humanity and that of society, and emerging into various forms of resistance against oppression.

The oppressed in particular struggle with their relation to the oppressor, and with emotions of vengeance and forgiveness. Simon Wiesenthal's book on the Jewish Holocaust, *The Sunflower: On the Possibilities and Limits of Forgiveness*, contains responses of over fifty people to the question: "You are a prisoner in a concentration camp. A dying Nazi soldier asks you for your forgiveness. What would you do?" When faced in real life with this very scenario, Mr. Wiesenthal himself fell silent and walked away. Other commentaries in *The Sunflower* express various personal and social dimensions of the encounter between oppressor and oppressed:

Smail Balic: One of the story's central concerns is the impassive societal reaction to transgression. Those who might appear uninvolved in the actual crimes, but who tolerate acts of torture, humiliation, and murder, are certainly also guilty. Looking away may be a comfortable but ultimately disastrous path, the effects of which are incalculable. (111)

Sven Alkalaj: [M]ust one forget before one can forgive? Without justice, there can never be reconciliation and real peace. (102–3)

Moshe Bejski: [The oppressed are] the emotionally and physically broken victims of those crimes, whose pain is too much to bear because of what they have done to him, his family, and his people. The victims were degraded, made to feel subhuman. (114)

Robert McAfee Brown: Never forgive, never forget. For if we forgive, it will be a sign to those in the future that they can act without fear of punishment, and that the universe has a moral escape valve labeled 'forgiveness' that permits evil not only to survive, but to thrive. On this reading, forgiveness becomes a 'weak' virtue, one that Christians seem particularly prone to champion, and one that always carries the possibility of condoning, rather than constricting, the spread of evil. (121)

Eugene Fisher: Placing [a victim] in this anguished position [to forgive] further victimizes him or her. (133)

The families of surviving victims are "emotionally and physically broken" (Wiesenthal 114) as a result of hate crimes.

Alienation, degradation, and dehumanization are experiences expressed by many of the survivors in this volume, such as the Laotian parents described by Misa Joo. Victims of racial violence all seem to experience a posttraumatic stress phase following hate crimes. A process of healing generally occurs in the aftermath, involving a recovery period for their emotional, psychological, and/or physical wounds. Doug Tang and Jia Ling powerfully describe their struggles with identity, depression, and anger. For some, it may take years to recover from the acts of racial violence. For others, the healing may never take place if their wounds are too deep. If the wounds are deep, forgiveness may be hard to achieve.

Discussions around forgiveness and hate crimes are now beginning to surface. Will the wife of Mr. Kao ever fully recover from her husband's tragic death? The fact that the police forbade her to administer first aid to her dying husband will, no doubt, trouble her for years. Has Vincent Chin's mother been able to forgive his murderers? Have any of the families of the other victims of hate crimes been able to forgive their perpetrators? Should they? What about the Asian American university students in New York who were beaten as security guards watched and did nothing? The silence of the security guards condoned those acts of violence. Will those students ever be able to forgive the security guards who chose not to defend them? Smail Balic's comments on indifference address this moral dilemma. His conclusion is that indifference leads to disastrous consequences. In this sense, the security guards, by remaining uninvolved, were also guilty for tolerating the acts of violence committed against the students.

The contributors to *The Sunflower* were divided over the issue of whether or not one should forgive perpetrators of violence. Certainly, forgiveness is not the complete and total answer for all cases of hate crimes or other acts of violence. Each case is different, as are the people involved. Moreover, many writers and activists want to resist the tendency to blame the victim in this culture. Cynthia Ozick, in *The Sunflower*, has this to say about forgiveness: "It forgets the victim. It blurs over the suffering and death. It drowns the victim. It cultivates sensitiveness towards the murderer at the price of insensitiveness toward the victim" (216). Referring to the indifference Balic speaks of, Ozick condemns the intelligent man of conscience who has allowed himself to "become a savage by deadening his humanity" (219).

Another factor seems to be the religion of the victim. Most Buddhists, such as the Dalai Lama (a contributor to Wiesenthal's volume), would be inclined toward forgiveness, as would some Christians. For Jews, the responses cover a broader range. In this book, Tang describes the influence of Gandhi and of philosophies of nonviolence. How would other survivors of anti-Asian violence respond to Mr. Wiesenthal's question? And what would atheists believe? If you take into account a person's political, ethical, and moral beliefs, the range of responses becomes wider still, and would be as varied as the human population itself.

Among the Asian American authors in this volume, the activism and resistance initiated by an experience of victimization also takes many forms. Mathur writes, "[W]ords and language (while perhaps not so overt as boots and fists) . . . are . . . acts of hate that help to maintain oppressive power structures." Mathur, Chow, and Watada have all found literary and artistic expression to be powerful tools in their own healing and for social change. Hwang and Yoshida have worked in the judicial system to reform U.S. social institutions, and Eric Mar has been active in community programs and social-justice movements. Misa Joo has reached out to victims on a very personal and emotional level.

What about the reformation of the oppressors? Again in *The Sunflower*, Deborah Lipstadt states that she has "yet to encounter a perpetrator who is actually seeking forgiveness" (196). Have any of the perpetrators of anti-Asian violence sought the forgiveness of their victims? The psychological background of Mr. Machado, the perpetrator in Mavis Lee's chapter, is brought to the fore in his trial: the strategy of the defense is to excuse and explain the crime, not to acknowledge it or seek forgiveness. In Yoshida's essay, the defendant only wrote a letter of apology to his lawyer and never directly addressed his hate-crime victims. Why? The question of the mentality of the perpetrator regarding forgiveness is compounded by Yoshida's observation, which I mentioned in the introduction but which bears repeating here, that every hate crime affects not only the targeted victim, but also the targeted community.

Some Americans and Canadians blame Japanese Americans and Japanese Canadians for their internment in concentration camps during World War II. Others state paternalistically that internment was intended for the safety of the internees themselves during wartime. Both of these rationales merely prevent understanding and acceptance on the part of the American and Canadian populations of the crimes against humanity that were committed by their countries against their own people. One need not create a chain of suffering in comparing this experience to the Jewish Holocaust to acknowledge that Asian Americans and Asian Canadians suffered tremendous losses emotionally, psychologically, physically, and financially when their homes and belongings were taken away from them by their respective governments. Despite the redress and reparations that have been made, some may never be able to fully recover from these dehumanizing and traumatic experiences. With racial violence and hate crimes, the long-lasting effects on the victims are multiplied many times.

During the final stages of preparation of this book, a hate crime occurred in the United States that received national attention. On April 28, 2000, a thirty-four-year-old immigration lawyer named Richard Baumhammers shot and killed five people in Pittsburgh, Pennsylvania: a Jewish woman, an Indian man, a Chinese, a Vietnamese, and a Black man. Baumhammers has been arraigned on charges of reckless endangerment, homicide, and one count of ethnic intimidation. When will we ever learn from our past mistakes? When will the violence stop?

In yet another case, Professor Lane Hirabayashi, at the University of Colorado, Boulder, received an anonymous death threat, filled with obscenities, on his campus voice mail last spring. The message was from a young man who was apparently dissatisfied with a grade. Dr. Hirabayashi teaches classes in Asian American studies at UCB. He transformed this disturbing event into a learning experience for his students by asking them to analyze the case to discover ways in which the situation could have been handled differently by the perpetrator and him.

In Wiesenthal's volume, Susannah Heschel, whose father is a rabbi, writes, "the blood of the innocent cries forever" (173). Heschel believes that the descendants of the Nazis should continue to "hear the cries of Jewish blood and thereby preserve their own humanity" (173). Similarly, the perpetrators of anti-

Asian violence should never forget the blood of people of Asian descent that has been spilled as a result of their unconscionable deeds.

Having experienced both subtle and overt forms of racial prejudice several times in my own life, one would think that I'd have grown numb to its effects by now. Instead, I have become only more determined to work toward ending or reducing the amount of hate crimes worldwide. It is my life's work. What is insidious about racism is that it destroys people's spirits. Blaming the victim only serves to reinjure the victim (as seen in Victor Hwang's chapter). In addition, we should reexamine the ill effects of slavery and colonization and the detrimental viewing of non-Whites as other or as inferior to Whites.

White supremacists and neo-Nazis need to see that human beings are the same all over the world. Their desires for an all-White world are not realistic, given that the world is populated mostly by people of Asian descent. They need to recognize that Hitler's genocidal fantasies ended tragically for him in his suicide. Hitler failed. Racists need to come to the realization that human beings are all interconnected on this planet. We need each other to survive. People all have the same needs and desires to live happy, fulfilled lives. Everyone wants to be loved and respected. All of the religious texts condemn violence and hatred. People need to look beyond the superficialities of race to see the humanity that lies within each of us, regardless of our religion, nationality, or race. Only by looking beyond issues of race, gender, ethnicity, religion, sexual orientation, and other falsely constructed dividers will we be able to survive as a species on this planet. Some former White supremacists have come to this realization and have reformed themselves. Only in this way will peace on earth be truly possible.

BIBLIOGRAPHY

Asian American Legal Defense and Education Fund. E-mail to author. 28 April 2000.
CBS News. "Baumhammer's Shootings in Pennsylvania." 29 April 2000.
Chan, Sucheng. *Asian Americans: An Interpretive History*. New York: Twayne, 1991.

Freire, Paulo. *Pedagogy of the Oppressed*. New York: Continuum, 1999.
Hirabayashi, Lane. "How a Death Threat Became an Opportunity to Connect with My Students." *The Chronicle of Higher Education*, 12 May 2000: B10.
Ryan, William. *Blaming the Victim*. New York: Vintage, 1976.
Wiesenthal, Simon. *The Sunflower: On the Possibilities and Limits of Forgiveness*. New York: Schocken, 1998.

Afterword

Mary-Woo Sims

The dedication by P. W. Hall and V. M. Hwang at the beginning of this book reads: "This book is dedicated to our parents, to our families, and to the past victims of hate crimes."

"Past victims of hate crimes." Don't we all hope that hate crimes will become a matter of the past? Having read the personal recollections of Americans and Canadians of Asian descent about hate and racism in their lives, will we all rededicate ourselves to preventing more hate crimes in the future? How do hate crimes occur? What is the root of this evil?

On November 16, 1999, the British Columbia Human Rights Commission, of which I am the chief commissioner, released a report titled *A Call to Action: Combatting Hate in British Columbia*. (November 16 incidentally is also the UNESCO International Day for Tolerance.) The commission views hate crime and hate activity as the extreme end of a continuum that begins with prejudice, stereotypes, and negative attitudes toward others based on race, place of origin, ancestry, color, sex, sexual orientation, religious beliefs, or other factors. The commission believes that our refusal, as a society, to accept and embrace difference and diversity is the root cause of prejudice and discrimination, which can lead to hate crimes and activities. Fear and ignorance too often fuel harmful attitudes toward others who are perceived to be different. Thus the foundation is laid for an intolerant and

179

hate-promoting community, rather than one that celebrates the diversity of its citizens and works to ensure all are included, respected, and treated with dignity.

Ironically, November 16, 1999, was also the same date on which sentences were handed down in the murder trial of young skinheads who had been charged with the murder of an elderly Sikh man, Nirmal Singh Gill. In 1998, five men, ranging in age from seventeen to twenty-five, were arrested for the murder of Gill, a sixty-five-year-old caretaker at a Sikh temple in Surrey, B.C., Canada. The suspects were members of a locally based skinhead group calling itself White Power, which is aligned with other White-supremacist groups, including the Northern Hammerskins and the Heritage Front.

Evidence suggests that only 5 percent of hate-motivated crimes are committed by members of organized hate groups. The fact that individuals with no apparent connection to hate groups commit 95 percent of the incidents shows the need to concentrate antihate initiatives across the entire community.

Also in B.C., we were shocked by the senseless beating and drowning death of Reena Virk, a fourteen-year-old, in November of 1997. About eight teenagers around seventeen years old, seven of them girls, were alleged to have taken part in the murder. None of the teenagers were associated with organized hate groups. According to newspaper accounts, Reena was "an overweight teen" who didn't fit in. Though the crime was initially described as an incident of "bullying gone wrong," we have come to understand that the reasons behind Reena Virk's murder were much more complicated. In her December 1997 article, "Reena Virk: The Erasure of Race," published by the FREDA Centre for Research on Violence against Women and Children at Simon Fraser University, Dr. Yasmin Jiwani provides a more in-depth analysis of why the murder occurred.

> Reena Virk could not "fit in" because she had nothing to fit in to. She was brown in a predominantly white society. She was supposedly overweight in a society which values slimness to the point of anorexia, and she was different in a society which values "sameness" and uniformity. And she was killed by those who considered her difference an affront to their sense of uniformity. Their power and dominance, legitimized by and

rooted in the sexism and racism of the dominant white culture and its attendant sense of superiority, was used to force her into submission—a submission that amounted to her death and erasure from society.

Dr. Jiwani continues, "In the public presentation of the murder, Reena suffered yet another erasure. While the daily papers plastered her picture on the front and back pages, no mention save one noted that Reena Virk died because of racism. Instead, the stories repeatedly stressed her lack of fit [*sic*], and her overweight appearance. The implicit message was that had she been white and had she been thin, she would have fit in, and there would have been no reason for her to be killed."

One evening, my partner and I had my nephew, fourteen, and my niece, seventeen, over for dinner. I can't recall now how we moved into the subject of racism, but my nephew, born in Canada of two parents of Asian (Chinese) background, told me that Chinese kids were still being referred to as "Chinks." Further, when his "friends" used the word *Chinks* to describe others, they'd often elaborate to my nephew that they didn't really mean him because he was "one of us." I asked my nephew how he felt. "Badly," he said, "but what can I do about it?" I was disappointed by that answer. I didn't agree with him that he couldn't do anything about it, but I also understood why he would conclude he couldn't do anything. Of course, we had a long talk about that. He knew that his friends' proviso that "Chink" really didn't apply to him because he was "one of us" was disingenuous. He also knew that he could do something about the name-calling, but that to speak out against it would likely result in his being isolated by his friends. I knew that I couldn't tell him what to do, so we talked. I hope that one day he will decide to speak up against racism, because he is already being hurt by it.

We all know what fuels the hate that leads to hate crimes. What are we doing about it? Most often, we call on governments and institutions to fight prejudice and hate. We call for tougher antihate legislation. We call for education. All these responses are helpful, but I believe that each individual can and should take individual actions against hate, bias, and prejudice in his or her daily life. We all bear an individual responsibility to create a society that is free from hatred and that promotes acceptance of diversity, peace, and understanding. We must ensure that all people feel that they belong and have a rightful place as citizens in this society. I intend to continue to do whatever I can to combat prejudice, discrimination, and hate. What about you?

Mary-Woo Sims
Chief Commissioner
British Columbia Human Rights Commission

Index

183

Index

About the Editors and Contributors

THE EDITORS

Patricia Wong Hall is a fourth-generation Chinese American who was born and raised in the United States. She has been the director, president, and adviser for four nonprofit organizations for Asian Americans since 1989. Her nonfiction works have appeared in *Asian Week* and other publications. She has given dozens of lectures on Asian American issues. In 1991, she won an award and a cash prize for a short story on anti-Asian violence. One of her poems, "Asian American Women's Blues," in *Skin Deep: Women Writing on Color, Culture, and Identity*, was reprinted by the Tufts University Women's Center in 1999. She teaches university courses on Asian religions, Asian American studies, and Asian American women (race and gender issues). She has been a community advocate since 1979. Ms. Hall is coproducing a play in 2001 on racial stereotypes and Asian American men titled *Exit the Dragon*.

Victor M. Hwang is the managing attorney of the Asian Law Caucus in San Francisco, directing its Hate Violence/Race Relations project. As part of his work, Mr. Hwang provides legal representation to victims of hate violence and police misconduct, conducts research and analysis of patterns and trends in anti-Asian violence, and is active in several diverse coalitions, including the Hate Violence Network, the Bay Area Hate Crimes Investigators Association, and the Retail Discrimination Committee. As part of the National Asian Pacific American Legal Consortium, Mr. Hwang is also a coauthor of its annual national audit on anti-Asian violence.

Mr. Hwang has also served as cocounsel on several impact litigation, and class-action lawsuits, including *Truong v. San Francisco Housing Authority* (challenging systematic failure to address racial violence against Southeast Asians in the housing developments), *Sutich v. Callahan* (challenging denial of benefits to legal permanent residents under welfare reform), *Yang v. Glickman* (challenging denial of benefits to Hmong veterans), and *Kao v. Rohnert Park* (seeking redress for a police killing that was based on a martial-arts stereotype).

The caucus is the nation's oldest civil-rights legal organization serving the Asian Pacific American population. The mission of the Asian Law Caucus is to promote, advance, and represent the legal and civil rights of the Asian Pacific Islander communities through a combination of direct legal services, community education, technical assistance to service providers, community organizing, and impact litigation. The caucus is a founding member of the National Asian Pacific American Legal Consortium based in Washington, D.C.

THE CONTRIBUTORS

Ritz Chow was four when she and her parents left Hong Kong and landed in Toronto on a cold winter night. She saw her first snowfall in the Riverdale neighborhood of Toronto. Her writing has appeared in Canadian feminist and poetry journals and in various anthologies, including *Swallowing Clouds: An Anthology of Chinese-Canadian Poetry* and *Piece of My Heart: A Lesbian of Colour Anthology.* Currently, she practices as a pharmacist and is examining identity politics within narratives of illness and disability for her M.A. research at Simon Fraser University, British Columbia.

Misa Kawai Joo is a third-generation Japanese American (*sansei*), a mother, and a middle-school teacher. She is also a third-generation teacher. Her grandmother, Misa Ota Kawai, was a teacher in Gifu-ken, Japan, in the early 1900s before immigrating with her husband, Shichiro Kawai, to dusty farmlands along the Snake River in southern Idaho. Her mother, Mary Kawai Joo, entered college after she was forty years old and taught for several years at Caldwell, Idaho, before retiring. Ms. Joo is uplifted by her students at the Jefferson Institute of Multicultural and International Education, a public school. Their deep commitment to a respectful and inclusive school community as a Racism Free Zone school and their creative, high energy give her hope. She, her husband, Will, and their high-school-age daughter, Maki, live in Eugene, Oregon.

Mavis K. Lee was an assistant United States attorney of the Central District of California in Los Angeles when she coprosecuted the case presented in "Hate Crime on the Internet: The University of California, Irvine, Case." Her current practice focuses on federal criminal prosecution of high-technology crimes.

Jia Ling was born in Brooklyn on October 27, 1969, a second-generation Chinese American. She grew up in Los Angeles (thereabouts), but possesses a great attitude about life nonetheless. She has a "cute but worthless" bachelor's degree in philosophy from the California State University of Fullerton. Ms. Ling believes in movement, things in themselves, and worshiping the moment. Ms. Ling is in love with words, music, fruit, and skin. She wants to use personal art as a fuller, juicier way of speaking. She loves her mother, her partner, and herself. "I had so much to say for this essay, but I had to cut the most depressing bits out. (I'm still like my mother that way.) The stories flowed from me like water, because I have been carrying them around for so long without giving them words. My life, my work, my awareness . . . it's all about patterns, the ones I've been given and the ones I make. This essay, for example, is all about the rhythms in home life being mirrored by the outside, the history of what's gone on before me and all the little parts we play, and when I come in and take over."

Eric Mar is a San Francisco attorney who teaches Asian American and ethnic studies at San Francisco State University. He is the past director of the Northern California Coalition for Immigrant Rights and served as the assistant dean and as a professor of law at New College of California School of Law from 1993 to 1997. Mr. Mar is a longtime board member of the Chinese Progressive Association and a founding member of API for CE (Asian Pacific Islanders for Community Empowerment) and the Institute for Multiracial Justice. He is active in the Asian Pacific American Labor Alliance (APALA) and a former shop steward for the SEIU (Service Employees International Union) Local 790. Mr. Mar is an elected member of the San Francisco Democratic County Central Committee and a board member of San Franciscans for Tax Justice and the Media Alliance. He became active in racial-justice work in the early 1980s with Davis Asians for Racial Equality (DARE) and the Chinese Progressive Association in San Francisco's Chinatown. Mr. Mar is also a commissioner on the San Francisco Board of Education. He currently lives with his wife, Sandra Chin Mar, a teacher, and their baby daughter in San Francisco's Richmond district.

Ashok Mathur is an antiracist educator and activist in Calgary. He teaches theory and humanities courses in the liberal studies department of the Alberta College of Art and Design. Mr. Mathur's research is based on critical race theory and he has published two books: *Loveruage: A Dance in Three Parts*, a poetic narrative around identity formation (1994), and *Once Upon an Elephant* (1999), a novel challenging assumptions of race and sexuality.

Doug A. Tang is a writer and screenwriter living in Austin, Texas. Interested readers may take a peek at his other works at www.arriveat.com/theitworks.

Terry Watada is an Asian Canadian writer living in Toronto. His published books include *Seeing the Invisible* (a children's biography of Dr. Irene Uchida; Umbrella Press, 1998), *Daruma Days* (a collection of short fiction; Ronsdale Press, 1997), *Bukkyo Tozen* (a history of Buddhism in Canada; HpF Press, 1996), and *A Thousand Homes* (poetry; Mercury Press, 1995). *A Thousand Homes* was short-listed for the 1995 Gerald Lampert Award for the best first book of poetry published in Canada. Mr. Watada's poem "Moon above the Ruins" was included in *Vintage 99*, an anthology of the best poems of the twelfth National Poetry Contest, sponsored by the League of Canadian Poets. Mr. Watada has four play productions to his credit: *Vincent* and *The Tale of a Mask*, by the Workman Theatre Projects, and *Mukashi Banashi* and *Mukashi Banashi II* (Japanese children's tales), by Japanese Folklore Productions. He has produced eight record albums of his music. His ninth, *Hockeynight in Chinatown*, with the Asian Canadian folk-rock band Number One Son, was released in the summer of 2000. He is currently working on a novel and on a play for Canadian Stage Productions.

Michelle Yoshida is an attorney practicing with the firm of Bledsoe, Cathcart, Diestel, and Pedersen, LLP, in San Francisco. Previously, Ms. Yoshida worked with the U.S. Commission on Civil Rights on a spectrum of diverse civil-rights issues, including affirmative action, hate crimes, Hawaiian sovereignty, health care, police practices, racial profiling, standardized testing, and zero tolerance. Following her experience with a hate crime, Ms. Yoshida continues to advocate for better enforcement of existing hate-crime statutes, the passage of stronger hate-crime legislation, and better education and coalitions of communities of color against hate crimes. Ms. Yoshida is a fourth-generation Japanese American.